For Orange and the States

The Army of the Dutch Republic, 1713–1772

Part I: Infantry

Marc Geerdink-Schaftenaar

Helion & Company

Helion & Company Limited
Unit 8 Amherst Business Centre
Budbrooke Road
Warwick
CV34 5WE
England
Tel. 01926 499 619
Fax 0121 711 4075
Email: info@helion.co.uk
Website: www.helion.co.uk
Twitter: @helionbooks
Visit our blog at http://blog.helion.co.uk/

Published by Helion & Company 2018
Designed and typeset by Mach 3 Solutions Ltd (www.mach3solutions.co.uk)
Cover designed by Paul Hewitt, Battlefield Design (www.battlefield-design.co.uk)
Printed by Henry Ling Limited, Dorchester, Dorset

The Dutch guards exercising at the Koekamp in The Hague, commanded by Colonel Jacob
van Kretschmar; painting by T.P.C. Haag, before 1770. (© Private Collection, with kind permission
of C.van Kretschmar).

ISBN 978-1-911512-15-8

British Library Cataloguing-in-Publication Data.
A catalogue record for this book is available from the British Library.

For details of other military history titles published by Helion & Company Limited, contact the
above address, or visit our website: http://www.helion.co.uk

We always welcome receiving book proposals from prospective authors.

Contents

Introduction

When it comes to the history of the Netherlands, the 18th century is usually not a popular subject for study. In particular, the military history of that period has long been neglected. The reason is for that is that the 18th century was essentially a period of decline. It forms a strong contrast with the 17th century, which has been, and still is, regarded as the Netherlands' Golden Age. At that time the Dutch Republic, independent since 1648 after the 80 Years War against Spain, was at the height of its power. A small, yet industrious nation of tradesmen, its ships sailed to all the far corners of the world, its cities bustled with trade, whilst new land was created by building dykes and polders. As the Dutch say: God created the earth and the universe in six days – except the Netherlands: that was made by the Dutch themselves.

The Republic in the 1700s, however, is regarded as a nation of spineless, decadent fops, with their powdered wigs and country estates along the Vecht. It is no small wonder that after the turbulent Napoleonic Wars, the newly created Kingdom of the Netherlands, desperate to present itself to the rest of Europe and eager to once again join the ranks of the major powers, would rather identify itself with the fierce men of Holland and Zeeland who, led by the Orange-Nassau dynasty, had gained their hard-fought independence, and had emerged as the nation of stout sailors and enterprising tradesmen of the Golden Age. So when once again independence was secured under the Orange-Nassau dynasty on the fields of Waterloo, the decline and demise of the Dutch Republic in the 18th century would therefore be pushed into the background, as merely an unpleasant memory. From now on, it was 'God, Fatherland and Orange' as far as everyone was concerned, and the 17th century was the ideal to which all Dutchmen would mirror themselves and their nation.

So when in 1935, the enterprising infantry lieutenant I.L Uijterschout decided to write a book, entitled *A Concise Summary of the Most Important Events in Dutch Military History* (*Beknopt Overzicht van de Belangrijkste Gebeurtenissen uit de Nederlandsche Krijgsgeschiedenis van 1558 tot Heden*), it is no surprise that the whole 18th century was only mentioned briefly: one page out of a total of 488 was all that he could spare on listing the wars between 1680 and 1787 – and most of the page relates how he 'merely wanted to limit the size of his work'. A short selected list of further reading suffices. Given the tone of the book, which is fanatically pro-Orange and in which the author time and again urges for more spending on the armed forces, it is exemplary of the negative attitude towards the history of the Dutch Republic during the 18th century.

As far as our knowledge of the army of the Dutch Republic itself is concerned, that is also a blind spot. To fill the void, a bold project was started in the early 20th century, resulting in a series of books called *The States Army 1568–1795* (*Het Staatse Leger 1568–1795*). Written by (among others) F.J.G. ten Raa, these volumes give detailed information about the organization of the States Army, the conflicts in which it was involved, the political and historical background, and so forth. The project ended quite abruptly in 1964, after the publication of Volume 3 of Part VIII. In 2009, the long awaited Part IX, written by the late H.L. Zwitser, was published – almost a century after the publishing of Part I and 50 years after the last publication of Part VIII. But where the first eight parts are about the period from its founding in 1568, until the end of the War of Spanish Succession in 1713 – 135 years in ten books – Part IX deals with the entire period from 1713 until the disbanding of the States Army in 1795. That is 135 years in 10 books (plus an atlas), compared to 82 years in one book. Since no less than three volumes, accompanied by an atlas, were needed just to describe the War of Spanish Succession in Part VIII, one volume about the 1713–1795 period seems meagre. Also lacking is information about uniforms: Part IX gives no information whatsoever, let alone illustrations.

So how come so little has survived the ages?

Especially throughout the 18th century, the army was never popular. Soldiers were regarded with disdain, something even foreign visitors were puzzled about: one visitor to the Netherlands in the 1760s described how he saw a peasant refusing to step aside for a soldier. At one point even, soldiers, as well as dogs, were not allowed in parks. For some part the common soldier had himself to blame for the bad reputation he and his comrades had amongst the populace, as described by a remarkable eyewitness, Maria van Antwerpen, a woman who posed as a soldier for a number of years (she enlisted three times), and was treated likewise:

> In Zeeland and Northern Holland, one follows the same habits in *Amourettes* in regard to those in the Military: when one wants to go courting a young daughter, one needs to go out in the evening, when it's dark, when they can be found in the streets and on the pavements by the dozens; but daytime is sacred, and no matter how polite one greets, a good soldier is not even looked at, in fear of a young maiden damaging her good name and reputation, concerns that are very much justified.

Also, the army was never as popular a subject for artists as the navy was; 17th and 18th century paintings usually depict famous sea battles from the wars against Britain, Spain and France, battles that secured many a victory over the enemies of the Republic and made it a maritime superpower. That changed during the 1780s, a time of great political tension in the Republic, when the many Patriotic Free Corps and newly raised Legions of the States Army, with their lavish and exotic uniforms, were catching the attention of painters and printmakers. There is a lot to find from the period after 1780, especially from the Napoleonic era, but any earlier information is scarce, although there were (and still are) some paintings, several portraits of officers, and even surviving pieces of uniform, stored in private collections, hung on castle walls, or stowed away in attics or depots of local museums.

By the end of the 19th century, there were initiatives to preserve as much of the Netherlands' military history as possible. The retired Major General of Artillery F.A. Hoefer gathered a large collection of military items in Castle Doorwerth during the end of the 19th and beginning of the 20th centuries, which served as his private military museum. The military painter J. Hoynck van Papendrecht set up his studio in the castle, and brought his private collection as well. Meanwhile, the retired cavalry officer Albert Carel, Baron Snouckaert van Schauburg, set up his own collection of military memorabilia. Having access to the court archive and library of Queen Wilhelmina, he studied several sources, and published a work on the flags and standards of the Dutch Army. In 1884, he acquired two small books, which combined would became known as the *Jassenboekje* ['Coats booklet' or 'Little book of Coats']. The first part contained a series of schematic drawings showing the uniforms of the Dutch army from somewhere around 1750–1760 to 1795. The second contained a similar series, showing the post-1795 uniforms of the army of the Batavian Republic. Snouckaert van Schauburg donated his collection to the *Krijgskundig Archief* (the Archive for Military Studies), together with a series of watercolours depicting the uniforms of the Dutch Army. These watercolours, each showing a soldier in full dress, are, despite their small size (19 x 11.5 cm., or 7.5 x 4.5 inches), highly detailed and of great artistic value. They were painted in 1773 by Duncan Macalaster (after 1786 known as Duncan Macalaster Loup), a junior officer in the Scots Regiment Marjoribanks. Snoukaert van Schauburg had acquired these in 1879.

These two collections, painstakingly gathered over the years, and containing a wealth of information, fell victim to the violence of World War II. In 1944, Castle Doorwerth was right in the middle of the fighting in Operation Market Garden, resulting in the destruction of the castle and the loss of most of the military collections of Hoefer and Hoynck van Papendrecht. The collection of Snouckaert van Schauburg was kept in a safe deposit in a bank, only to be taken out for studies by members of the Archive for Military Studies. It was during one of those studies that the location of the Archive, the Nieuwe Uitleg in The Hague, was bombed by the RAF on March 3 1945 and completely destroyed. Of their entire collection, only the *Jassenboekje* and the watercolour series could be saved from the flames. What little that is left is now preserved in the National Institute for Military History (NIMH) and the new National Military Museum in Soesterberg. Studies in watercolour, paint, pencil, or ink by artists like Hoynck van Papendrecht and others, give some idea of the numerous pieces of clothing and artefacts that were sadly lost.

The 18th century is slowly but surely gaining more interest, and not just from the odd history buff. One author who is placing the military history of the Dutch Republic in the 18th century in the spotlights is Dr Olaf van Nimwegen, an expert who has dug up vast amounts of information from different archives, and who has written several books on the Dutch Republic during the 17th and 18th centuries. Given the enormous amount of study already undertaken by him, it will not come as a surprise that his works will be mentioned a lot in this book.

Whereas Van Nimwegen has written extensively on the history of the army of the Dutch Republic, the idea for this book is to present specific information about the appearance of the army in the years between the Peace of Utrecht in 1713 and the uniform regulations of 1772. As has been said, little is preserved, and sources are scarce, but what is available is gathered here for the first time for an audience outside the Dutch-speaking countries. A large part will be dedicated to the War of the Austrian Succession (1740–1748), the last major European conflict before the French Revolutionary Wars in which the Army of the Dutch Republic played a large, albeit often neglected, part.

Timeline

1713	Peace of Utrecht ends the War of Austrian Succession.
1715	Third Barrier Treaty between the Republic, Britain, and Austria. An auxiliary corps of 6,000 men is sent to Britain to support the campaign against the Jacobite rebels.
1716–1717	Great Assembly in order to negotiate state reforms.
1717	Triple Alliance between Britain , France, and the Republic.
1718	Quadruple Alliance between France, Austria, and Britain, with an invitation to the Republic. The seven-year-old Prince of Orange is elected as Stadholder of Groningen.
1719	French invasion of Spain. 2,000 Dutch troops under Major General Keppel sent to Britain to help quell a Jacobite rising; Dutch troops fight at Glen Shiel.
1720	Peace between Spain and the Quadruple Alliance.
1722	Prince of Orange elected Stadholder of Gelderland and Drenthe.
1724	Treaty of Vienna between Austria and Spain.
1725	Treaty of Hannover between Britain, France and Prussia, later joined by the Republic.
1726	Augmentation of the Army by 9,500 men.
1728	Regulations for the Army regarding drill reviewed and laid down to promote uniformity within the army.
1728–1729	Congress of Soissons.
1729	Treaty of Seville between Britain, France, Spain, and the Republic. The Republic mobilises an army to possibly aid Hannover in its conflict with Prussia.
1731	The Republic reconciles with Austria and enters the Treaty of Vienna.
1732	Military manoeuvres at Oosterhout.
1733	Death of King-Elector Augustus II of Poland and Saxony; beginning of the War of Polish Succession. The Republic signs a Neutrality Convention and offers, with Britain, to act as mediators.
1735–1738	Peace negotiations, later ratified in the Treaty of Vienna.

1740	Death of Emperor Charles VI; King Frederick II of Prussia invades Silesia, thereby beginning the War of Austrian Succession.
1742	The Republic enters the War of the Austrian Succession.
1743	A Dutch corps is sent to Germany, but arrives too late to take part in the campaign. Auxiliary corps of 6,000 men is sent to Britain.
1744	French invasion of the Austrian Netherlands. French army captures Courtrai, Menin, Ypres, and Veurne. Allied army marches into France, but the campaign is a failure.
1745	Dutch garrison at Tournai is besieged by the French. French victory over the Allied army at Fontenoy. Jacobite Rebellion under Charles Edward Stuart compels Britain to withdraw part of its army. Another Dutch auxiliary corps is sent to Britain.
1746	Allied defeat at Rocoux. The French take Mons, Charleroi, Namur, and other garrisons in rapid succession and control the Austrian Netherlands. Jacobite Army defeated at Culloden Moor.
1747	French invasion of the Republic. Allied defeat at Lauffeld. Bergen op Zoom besieged and taken by a French force under Löwendahl. Prince Willem IV becomes Captain-General and Stadholder of all provinces. Immediate augmentation of the army.
1748	Maastricht captured by a French force under de Saxe. Peace of Aix-la-Chapelle ends the War of the Austrian Succession. Austria is given back its possessions in the Netherlands.
1749	New exercise and manuals for the infantry.
1750	Expedition to Suriname by a combined expeditionary force.
1751	Death of Stadholder Willem IV, his son becomes Stadholder Willem V.
1752	Reorganization in order to make the army more cost-effective and efficient. New uniform regulations for the armed forces.
1756	Seven Years War begins. The Republic remains neutral.
1759	Founding of the Armouries at Culemborg. Ludwig Ernst, Duke of Brunswick-Wolfenbüttel, becomes regent for the young Stadholder Willem V.
1763	Peace of Hubertusburg ends the Seven Years War Expedition to Berbice in order to quell the slave revolt.
1765–1778	Slave revolt led by guerrilla leader Boni erupts in Surinam (First Boni War).
1769	Military camp at Breda.
1771	New exercise and manuals for the army.
1772	New uniform regulations for the armed forces. Marine Regiment sent to Surinam to quell the slave revolt.

1

The Dutch Republic, 1713–1740

The United Netherlands

The Dutch Republic, also known as the United Provinces or Republic of the United Netherlands, had declared independence from Spain in 1581, and became truly independent after the Peace of Münster in 1648. By then, the Republic was already a major power with a thriving economy, a large, modern army, and a mighty fleet that had conquered one of the largest colonial empires. The *Vereenigde Oost-Indische Compagnie* (VOC; United East India Company) was the worlds' first multinational, with stockholders buying shares to have a piece of the winnings in the spice trade. Most wealth came, however, from the trade in wood with the North, from grazing cattle that migrated from Denmark and Germany to Holland each year, and from expertise in shipbuilding and water management: large parts of northern Germany, Poland and the Baltic states were drained, thanks to Dutch expertise, turning swamps into agricultural lands, whilst Dutch sailors, seamen, and shipwrights travelled across Europe and helped build and man fleets in Britain, Sweden, and later Russia.

The Republic was a confederation of semi-independent provinces, every province having a parliament, the *Staten* (States). The overall government was the *Staten Generaal* (States General), to which every province sent representatives. There were eight provinces: Holland, Zeeland, Utrecht, Gelderland, Overijssel, Friesland, and Groningen (or *Stad en Lande*; the town of Groningen and the surrounding lands); the eighth province Drenthe was very poor, so since it was exempt from taxes, it was not represented in the States General. Individual provinces fended for themselves, with only foreign policy and military matters being handled by the States General. Within each province, every town or district also had a lot of autonomy. Local magistrates could therefore have a lot of influence on the affairs of state: the objections of the town of Dordrecht against sending troops to help Austria in 1743 led to seemingly endless negotiations. One can imagine though that a city like Amsterdam, which paid half of the taxes of the province Holland – which in turn paid for the largest part of the army of the States General – had more to say than, for instance, Franeker in Friesland or Harderwijk in Gelderland. Nevertheless, it was common knowledge that this autonomy had a crippling effect on decision making, resulting in months of endless debates and awaiting the approval of town councils on matters of State. An attempt was made in 1716 to negotiate state reforms, where the autonomy of the towns and provinces would be limited, and which would lead to a more centralized government under the States General, but this Great Assembly was dissolved the next year as it reached no conclusion.

Holland, Zeeland and Utrecht were the richest and most important provinces; Holland was so dominant that it led to the Republic being often referred to as Holland (not only then, but even now). The Republic had also been assigned control over a number of border territories, known as the *Generaliteitslanden* (Generality Lands). These were Staats-Brabant (today the province of Noord-Brabant), Staats-Vlaanderen (present day Zeeuws-Vlaanderen), Staats-Limburg (the area around Maastricht) and Staats-Oppergelre (the area around Venlo).

In theory, there was no head of state. The main executive officials in the Republic were the *Raadpensionaris* – a title that roughly translates as Grand Pensionary –and the *Stadhouder* (Stadholder or Steward), a title derived from *Stedehouder*, one who rules 'instead' (*in stede*) of the King, and comparable to a Lord Lieutenant (also from *lieu*, 'instead' and *tenant*, 'holder'). The first was a sort of prime minister, whilst the second was more of a military leader, concerned with the safety and security in the province. Every province could elect a *Raadpensionaris* and a Stadholder. In reality, the *Raadpensionaris* of Holland was regarded as the most important political official. The Stadholder, who was the commander of the armies of the United Provinces, was in general regarded as the head of state. Only during the two Stadholderless eras (1650–1672, and 1711–1747) was the *Raadpensionaris* regarded as such, as there was no Stadholder elected in all seven provinces. The title was made hereditary after 1672 in some provinces, and finally in all provinces for the Orange-Nassau dynasty in 1747.

The great influence of the House of Orange-Nassau on the politics of the Dutch Republic led to a strong division of the Dutch into two main groups: one side were the Orangists, the supporters of the Prince of Orange-Nassau and his election to the title of Stadholder; the other side were the Republicans who wanted to get rid of the old feudal structure and create a true republic. The Republicans consisted for the most part of the rich middle and upper classes that took office in the provincial States, called *Regenten* (Regents). The Orangists mainly consisted of the lower classes. Prince Willem IV could rely on support in the more rural provinces of Friesland, Overijssel, Groningen, and Gelderland (where he was elected Stadholder), whilst in Holland (and especially the council of Amsterdam), Utrecht, and Zeeland the Republicans tried to keep the Prince out of any state affairs. The army, a bulwark of the Dutch nobility, as well as foreign nobility (to whom the idea of a Republic was quite unusual), was always a strong supporter of the Orangist cause, and the Regents feared the Stadholder would try a coup with the help of the army; Prince Willem II had attempted it in 1650, which had led to the first Stadholderless period. But as soon as the Republic was in danger, the lower classes and the army would call for the return of a Prince of Orange, and the Republicans would be swept aside. In 1787, it even led to civil war, in which Prussia intervened to reinstate Willem V to his office as Stadholder.

This vehement struggle, fought out in scores of pamphlets, in papers, from pulpits and even in the streets, lasted throughout the 18th century, and greatly divided the Republic on every level; it would prove to have a destructive effect on the governing of the Republic, and finally end in 1795, when the old Republic of the United Netherlands was abolished and the Orange dynasty fled into exile. The constitution of the Batavian Republic would unify the provinces into one state under one centralised government, thus ending the autonomy and influence of the provincial states and town councils.

The Wars of 1672–1713

The year 1672 is still known in the Netherlands as the *Rampjaar* (Disaster Year). The Dutch Republic which had arisen from the turmoil of the Dutch Revolt (1568–1648), was now surrounded by a coalition of Britain, France, Münster, and Cologne. The French army invaded the territory of the Republic, and even reached as far as Utrecht in the heart of it. The Dutch however, set up a defensive line by flooding low lying areas. This *Waterlinie* (Water Line), too deep to cross by an army, but too shallow to cross by boat, ground the French invasion to a halt. The armies of Münster and Cologne tried desperately to get past the Dutch forces in the north, but without much success. At sea, the combined British and French fleets were kept at bay by the Dutch fleet under legendary commanders like Michiel Adriaansz. de Ruyter. In North America, the Dutch even recaptured New York, their former colony New Amsterdam. After some fierce fighting, the war ended in 1674, although the French kept up the hostilities until 1678. Having defeated the combined fleets of Britain and France, and driven back the invading armies, the war is regarded as the zenith of Dutch military prowess. But despite the success of the Dutch against the coalition, it had stretched the resources and capabilities of the Republic beyond what it could endure. Locked between a major land power – France – and a major sea power – Britain   it had to uphold both a strong fleet and a large army, a task that was virtually impossible. The economy had suffered a crippling blow, from which it would not soon recover. Unknown to the people at the time, it can now safely be stated that the Golden Age of the Dutch Republic had ended, and this would be a blueprint for whatever lay in the future.

One outcome of the war was the return of the Orange dynasty back to the title of Stadholder. Willem III was called upon to become military commander and ruler of the Dutch Republic. After the Glorious Revolution, he would become King of Great Britain as well, leading both nations against France during the Nine Years War. That ended with the Treaty of Rijswijk in 1697, by which France had to return the territories it had gained. The Treaty of Rijswijk however would prove to be no more than an armistice, for in 1700, the last Habsburg King of Spain died. A year later, the War of the Spanish Succession broke out. Willem III however died after a fatal accident in 1702; the Dutch Republic entered a second Stadholderless Period. Anti-Orangist, republican factions, usually not too keen on spending vast amounts of money on a large standing army, seized power, but contrary to what Louis XIV expected, they did not sue for peace. If the Spanish Netherlands was to fall into French hands, it was feared that this would lead to the downfall of Dutch trade. Thus, the Republic, alongside England and Austria, entered the war in 1702, and an Anglo-Dutch expeditionary force was sent to Spain immediately. The Dutch were more concerned, though, about the threats on their borders, and diverted their attention to the barrier towns in the south and the eastern border along the Meuse.

Hard fighting in the Spanish Netherlands, such as at Ramilies (1706) and Oudenaarde (1708), resulted eventually in the French being driven away by the Dutch and English. The Dutch Republic played a major part in this conflict, not only by bringing a large army into the field, which grew to 119,000 men in 1712, but also providing funds to support allied armies. However, the conduct of the Duke of Marlborough, the famous English commander, led in the end to the Dutch forces bearing the brunt of the fighting. And when the Peace of Utrecht was signed in 1713, the English had secured for themselves a separate treaty with France, thus carrying off most of the spoils of the war. The Dutch had proven to be masters in the field, but poor negotiators. With the economy having suffered again greatly from the war, and the Republican factions in power, the Dutch Republic once again reduced the size of its army from 112,000 – mostly German subsidy troops – to a bare minimum of 40,000 men, whilst retreating behind its barriers and opting for a policy of armed neutrality.

The Barrier Treaties
Even before the end of the 80 Years War, the States General acknowledged that the greatest enemy was no longer Spain, but France. The Spanish Netherlands (largely present day Belgium), always the battleground where France sought to expand its territory, were a troublesome jewel in the Spanish crown. It became clear that Spanish forces in the Spanish Netherlands were scarce, and when the war would inevitably be resumed again, it would take too long for Spain to have an army in position to ward off any French invasion, and French troops would again march up to the borders of the Republic. A permanent force was needed to be at the ready.

And so, a first 'Barrier Treaty' was signed in 1698; it was not an official treaty between two countries, but merely a negotiation between the two army commanders Stadholder-King Willem III and the Spanish governor, Maximilian II of Bavaria, agreeing winter quarters for their troops at the end of a campaign. A Dutch force of 22 infantry battalions was garrisoned in eight Spanish fortresses, placed under Spanish command; these could be sent back the Republic at any time if the Spanish King had no desire for them any more. With the Dutch troops stationed in Ath, Mons, Charleroi, Courtrai, Luxembourg, Namur, Nieuwpoort and Oudenaarde, the war would stay outside of the territory of the Republic.

When Charles II of Spain died, the grandson of the Sun King, Philip of Anjou, ascended to the Spanish throne. For Willem III, it was unacceptable that the Spanish Netherlands would come under French influence, let alone that the French and Spanish crowns would be united. The Barrier Treaty proved useless, as in 1701 French troops, aided by the Spanish commanders, entered the eight barrier towns and captured the 22 battalions without firing

a shot. The Republic, Britain and Austria entered the Second Grand Alliance, to regain the Spanish Netherlands and thus separate the republic and France. The States General demanded that Mons, Charleroi, Damme, Dendermonde, Luxembourg, Roermond, Stevensweert, Saint-Donatien and Venlo would be handed over into power of the Republic – that is, with a Dutch garrison, under Dutch command, with the possibilities to strengthen, dismantle or move these towns and fortifications, and have provisions and ammunition delivered to them, if so desired by the States General. This barrier would be the main goal of the States General during the War of Spanish Succession: a barrier, as the Secretary to the Council of State Adriaan van der Hoop would write,

> [N]ot dependant on another nation, who would neglect these, but occupied by troops of the State, and in which the State would find assurance, since experience has taught that the Spaniards had these fell into decay out of incapacity and neglect, and that these had been sold and delivered to France by the Bavarian Elector.

After the major Allied victory at Ramilies on 23 May 1706, the States General had achieved its goal, but was persuaded by Britain to continue the war. It agreed, on the condition that the whole of the Spanish Netherlands would be part of the Barrier, including Oostende and Dendermonde, which had been occupied by British troops and were of vital political and economic importance to Britain. Britain protested, but with the war still raging on three years later, Britain agreed and the first Barrier and Succession Treaty of

A *'Corps de Garde'*, or watch room, by Cornelis Troost, 1748. Troost made several of these paintings, but studies have shown that the uniforms depicted bear no resemblance to existing units. Nevertheless, these paintings give an impression of the military fashion of the States Army. (Rijksmuseum)

29 October 1709 between the two Sea Powers guaranteed a 'double barrier' in the Spanish Netherlands: one outward barrier against France, one inward to govern the Spanish Netherlands as the States General saw fit. In return, the Republic would support the accession of the House of Hannover to the British throne.

The Treaty of Rastatt saw the Spanish Netherlands handed over to Austria, who was not so keen on the Republic's influence there. Before the Third Barrier Treaty was in effect, as stipulated in the Peace of Utrecht, Austrian troops marched into Brabant and Flanders, despite protests from the Republic. Britain supported the Republic's claims, as it was faced with the Jacobite Rising in 1715, and to which the Republic immediately sent a force of 6,000 men to support the Hanoverian succession. The Third Barrier Treaty of 1715 soon came to pass after that, stipulating that 12,000 Dutch troops and 18,000 Austrian troops would be garrisoned in the now Austrian Netherlands, whilst Austria would pay a yearly subsidy of 1.25 million guilders, half of the cost of maintaining the garrisons and fortifications needed. The Barrier combined the forces of the Republic, Britain, and Austria. It was not only the cornerstone of the Republic's military strategy against France, it also had the Republic gain a lot of economic influence in the Austrian Netherlands.

Campaigns in England and Scotland

The Republic was eager to send troops to help defeat the Jacobites, as doing so secured British support for the Barrier Treaty. Indeed, George I was very grateful for the immediate sending of an auxiliary corps, as expressed in the comment of the British envoy for the negotiations, Charles, 2nd Viscount Townsend:

> This great & remarkable instance of the States friendship & and concern for him will lay a lasting obligation upon his majesty, who will, you may depend on it, in return favour & support them upon all occasions, & as a proof of his intentions, he has ordered me to write to Count Cöningseck on the subject of ye Barrier in the strongest terms & entirely to the satisfaction of ye States.

The expeditionary force under command of Lieutenant General Van der Beke, consisted of seven regiments of infantry and a regiment of dismounted dragoons. The force was split up, with 3,000 men landing in Hull and the other 3,000 in London, where the troops were heartily received by the inhabitants. The troops marched north, towards Edinburgh. Provisions were excellent and morale was good, despite the long marches in bad winter weather. From Edinburgh, the troops marched towards Perth, where the 'Old Pretender' James Francis Edward Stuart had arrived on December 9 and a substantial Jacobite force of about 6,000 men had gathered. The Jacobites however were severely disheartened after the battle of Sherrifmuir (November 13), where they were unable to defeat the Government forces, despite outnumbering them 3 to 1, and were chased north and dispersed north of Aberdeen. That same day, a Jacobite force at Inverness surrendered, while the next day, another force was defeated at Preston (9–14 November). The States troops then took up quarters in the area around Montrose and Dundee until April

1716, when the troops were ordered to leave Scotland and return to England. In August, the auxiliary corps was transported back to the Republic.

In 1717, Spanish ambitions in the Mediterranean had led to a conflict with Britain. To prevent a British landing on the Iberian Peninsula, an invasion to initiate a Jacobite rising was planned in 1719: first, a landing with 300 Spanish Marines in Scotland that would bring arms and try to gather a Jacobite force; and second, a landing of the main force of 7,000 men in the South of England or Wales. The main force set sail in March, but was caught in a storm on the 29th, forcing the Spanish ships back into harbour. Unaware of what happened to the fleet, the marines landed on April 13 and set up their headquarters in Eilean Donan Castle. The highlanders however were not keen to take up arms again, and waited for news of the Spanish invasion in the south. After having marched around for more than a month in order to stir up the locals and gather a Jacobite force, the Spanish now realised that the main force would never come. By then, the government forces, including an expeditionary force of 2,000 men under the command of Major General Keppel sent by the States General, had come from Inverness on June 5 to stop them.

The Spanish and the Jacobites had taken up defensive positions in the hills, 18 km from Eilean Donan near the narrows of Glen Shiel. On 10 June, the Government forces advanced against the Jacobite positions after a bombardment by mortar batteries. Huffel's Regiment was part of the right wing of the Government forces and advanced up the hill against the Jacobites. The highlanders, badly provisioned and outnumbered, fled from their positions. The Spanish troops in the centre were now abandoned and had no other option than to retreat uphill. Three hours after the battle began, they surrendered; they were taken to Edinburgh and returned to Spain in October. The States' auxiliary corps returned home later that year.

Shifting Alliances

The outcome of the War of Spanish Succession has long been regarded as the end of the Republic as a major European power. Although a period of decline had set in after the Treaty of Rijswijk, and the Peace of Utrecht had been a major disappointment, the Dutch Republic still held its place among the European powers because of its economic wealth. Certainly those in power and in the army did not feel as if it was the beginning of the end. Despite its policy of neutrality in the coming years, it would be clear in 1740 that, although reluctant to enter the War of Austrian Succession, it would still be able to provide funds for one of the largest armies in Europe. The Republic managed to stay out of other conflicts in the first decades of the 18th century (apart from sending the small expeditionary forces to England and Scotland). But the threat of war was always imminent, and the alliance between the Republic, Britain, and Austria was not always that solid. The Republic therefore signed an 'everlasting defensive treaty' with France, guaranteeing the safety and neutrality of the Dutch garrisons in the Austrian Netherlands and the territory of the Republic.

Whereas the Republic would benefit from peace, Britain, and more specific Hannover, had more to gain by war. With its eyes fixed on the

Grenadier during the Battle of Malplaquet, detail of a print by Van Huchtenburg, 1726. (Rijksmuseum)

Swedish possessions in Verden and Bremen, Britain entered the Great Northern War in 1717. There was discussion in the Republic whether to join the Quadruple Alliance of Britain, Austria and France (the fourth place being reserved for the Republic), which soon declared war on Spain. It did not help that the Austrian Netherlands had also refused to pay the subsidy according to the Third Barrier Treaty and had to be persuaded to do so. When in 1720 the war ended, the other powers were in no need for the Republic to enter the Quadruple Alliance any more. Tensions between the Sea Powers and Austria rose after the founding of the *Kaiserlichen und Königlichen Indischen Kompanie*, or the Oostende Company, by Austria for the spice trade in the East Indies. Britain feared that the Oostende Company would be a guise under which Jacobite sympathisers, who were active in the Company, would again launch another invasion.

Now, the Amsterdam merchants certainly would not have objected had the VOC taken action against the ships of the Oostende Company, since it could wage war independently in the East Indian theatre; but the Oostende Company was protected by Austria itself, which would mean that if the VOC attacked the Oostende Company ships, it would surpass the States General, and the whole affair could spiral out of control. The *Raadpensionaris* Van Hoornbeek and Secretary to the Council of State Van Slingeland both urged Amsterdam to calm down, telling it and the VOC to act only if the safety of the Republic could be guaranteed.

A most unwelcome shift in the balance in Europe was the alliance between Austria and Spain in 1724. As a response to that alliance, Britain, Prussia and France signed the treaty of Hannover, inviting the Republic to join. The provinces debated about what to do: the Republic had little to gain from entering the Treaty of Hannover, but the Oostende Company could seriously damage Dutch trade. The Republic was therefore careful what to do next. Holland voted in favour of joining, but only after the town of Dordrecht consented. In 1726, Friesland and Zeeland consented as well, and in the end only Utrecht and Groningen had not yet decided on the matter. By then, Britain had enough of the delay. When the States General finally overruled Utrecht and the Republic entered the alliance, Prussia had stepped out and joined the Vienna Alliance. In the end, Austria decided the Oostende Company was not worth vexing the Sea Powers. The alliance with Spain ended in 1729, resulting in Spain entering into an alliance with Britain and France in the Treaty of Seville. When this treaty proved to be short lived, the Republic sought to reconcile once again with Austria. Since both the Republic and Britain had more to fear from Prussia, the three powers entered the Second Vienna Treaty (1731). The Oostende Company was disbanded.

Amsterdam, now free from unwelcome competition from Oostende, demanded that the army be reduced again, but the city of Leiden and the States of Zeeland urged for a strong army to impress the Prussians, who were seen as a threat on the eastern border. To impress Prussia, military manoeuvres were to be held in 1732 in Oosterhout in Staats-Brabant, consisting of 13 infantry battalions and 24 cavalry squadrons, with artillery totalling 10,000 men. The manoeuvres, however, showed that the army was in a sorry state, but Amsterdam still demanded the army to be reduced, and by the end of the year it was decided to reduce the army by 10,000 men – 500 more than the number of the augmentation a few years earlier. However, this reduction was most unwelcome, since a series of incidents in regard to aggressive recruiting by Prussian recruiting officers led to increasing tension with Prussia, whilst war between Austria and France over the succession to the Polish throne became more and more imminent. Britain affirmed its support of the Republic by offering to deny passage of Prussian troops through Hannover, and the aid of a force of 6,000 British and 6,000 German troops.

Nevertheless, it took Austrian pressure to relieve this tension in the end. Amsterdam and now also Leiden had to be persuaded to agree with keeping the 10,000 men in service by presenting them a worst case scenario: with Austria withdrawing half its troops from the Austrian Netherlands into Luxembourg and being occupied in Poland, and Britain unwilling to take sides in the upcoming Polish conflict, the French could be near the borders by winter. A treaty with France safeguarding the neutrality of the Republic could take this threat away. But the States of Gelderland saw it as a means to alienate the Republic from Austria, and were waiting for an Austrian response on the matter. A survey along the garrisons in the Austrian Netherlands, conducted on behalf of the States General, made it painfully clear Austria had severely neglected these garrisons: Mons had only 1,500 men where 8,000 were needed, Charleroi needed 5,000 but only had 300, just as Ath, that needed at least 4,000. And whatever soldiers available were in such a sorry state that they mostly 'not even resembled soldiers'. The conclusion was that the Republic, despite its support of Austria, was not to blame if it remained neutral in the upcoming conflict. The report persuaded Gelderland to agree with a treaty with France, which was signed in November 1733; it secured not only the neutrality of just the Barrier towns, but of the whole of the Austrian Netherlands: the Republic would not meddle in the affairs between France and Austria, and if Austria planned to start an offensive from the Austrian Netherlands into Frenchs territory, the Republic would do its utmost to persuade her not to do so. Meanwhile, the Republic and Britain had strengthened their relationship when Stadholder Prince Willem IV of Orange married King George II's eldest daughter Anna of Hannover.

All this was a severe blow for Austria, who had hoped the Republic would enter the war, and who laid the blame for Britain's neutrality with the Republic. Secretary to the Council of State Van Slingeland offered for the Sea Powers to act as mediators, which Austria declined, even though its situation became more and more precarious. In the end, France and Austria became weary of the war, and in the end a peace treaty was signed in 1738. Van Slingeland was heralded as the man who had kept the Republic out of the war that Austria had started so recklessly. Nevertheless, he warned that in the future, war might lay ahead and the Republic might not stay out of it for very long. The alliance between the Sea Powers and Austria was artificial, as there were no religious, cultural, or economic ties between the countries, and what brought them together was a common enemy. For Austria, it became painfully clear that it could not blindly trust its allies, and she began considering the possibility of an alliance with what was the other great Catholic power in Europe.

2

Entering the War of the Austrian Succession, 1740–1744

War Erupts in Europe

Charles VI, Emperor of the Holy Roman Empire, King in Germany, King of Hungary, Bohemia, Croatia and Serbia, Archduke of Austria, Duke of Luxembourg, Brabant, Limburg, Lothier, and Milan, Count of Namur, Flanders, and Hainaut, ruled over much of Europe. But for all his might, his main concern was that he had no male heir. He had sought allies to sign the Pragmatic Sanction, a treaty that would secure the throne for his eldest daughter Maria Theresia. All the major European states had given their support to the Pragmatic Sanction, albeit at some cost: Charles had to give up Lorraine, have the Oostende Company disbanded, and make commitments to Russia and Saxony which ultimately saw Austria fighting France and Spain in the War of the Polish Succession.

Britain was heading for a conflict with Spain that began with the boarding of the British merchant ship *Rebecca* by the Spanish *guarda costas* off the coast of Florida in 1731. The Spanish accused the British of smuggling in the Spanish Americas, and therefore had these coast guards, who were nothing more than privateers, board and search British merchant ships. Thus Robert Jenkins, captain of the *Rebecca*, was accused of being a smuggler by the Spanish captain Fandiño. And to make sure the British got the message, Fardiño cut off the ear of the unfortunate British captain, threatening to do the same to King George II if he dared to strike back. The boarding and searching of British vessels was a severe breach of international law in itself, but this incident, along with several others, led to growing tension, and when all diplomatic means had run out, a war broke out in 1739, which a century later would be named after that now famous severed body part of Captain Jenkins.

For the Republic, which had opted for a policy of neutrality, the actions of the Emperor and the tension between Britain and Spain made the threat of being dragged into a conflict all the more worrying. It was however vital not to let France become too powerful. The defeats that Austria suffered in Italy, and in the east against the Turks, weakened her position in Europe and could tip the balance in favour of France, whilst France would certainly not sit idly by if Spain was involved in a war. This called for an augmentation of the army and navy; a petition was sent to the Provinces in January 1740 for an expansion of the army by 11,000 men, mostly infantry and some dismounted dragoons. It took months for the petitions to be sent back, which was terribly embarrassing for the Republic: Zeeland and Groningen had objected most about the way this augmentation was to be paid for. Finally, in August, the petitions were agreed upon by all the Provinces, and not a moment too soon, for in October, Emperor Charles VI died. France and others immediately called out their support for another candidate for the Imperial crown, Prince-elector Charles Albert of Bavaria. It was however not France, but the new Prussian King Frederick II who started the war, by entering Silesia on December 16 at the head of an army of 27,000 men. As the Secretary to the States General François Fagel wrote when he heard the news:

> It seems the king, when he ascended to the crown, received a splendid and numerous body of troops, and a fortune in cash, and thus concluded he has no equal […], and that he is therefore free to undertake whatever he so pleases.

Despite protests and anti-British propaganda from the French through their ambassador in The Hague, Gabriël Jacques de Salignac, Marquis de Fénelon (1688–1746), the States General announced another augmentation of the army, this time of 9,000 men. Anti-Prussian sentiments were rife in the Republic, although no one was willing to immediately come to the aid of Maria Theresia: with France posing a possible threat to the Austrian Netherlands, sending an auxiliary corps to the aid of the Austrians would weaken the Barrier.

The Republic negotiated with Britain in January 1741 about how best to react to the Prussian aggression. Britain considered Prussia to be a threat to Hannover and therefore wanted the Republic to guarantee to send a corps of 5,000 men to defend it. With the War of the Spanish Succession in mind – in which the Dutch Republic bore the brunt of the conflict, and Britain reaped the benefits of the peace treaty – the States were reluctant to commit themselves to organise an army corps for the defence of Hannover, because once the Republic was involved into the conflict, it would have to fight until the bitter end: unlike Britain, which could retreat from the continent across the Channel. Furthermore, asking for approval of organising such a force would take a very long time, since the proposal would have to be signed and ratified by all the Provincial States. The overall conclusion was that as long as France remained out of the conflict, there was no need for the Republic to get involved, and the whole matter could be resolved through diplomacy. The following was decided that: 1) the Republic would only send troops if King George II would guarantee to send troops for the defence of the Republic if needed; 2) to show the Sea Powers were still resolved to stand behind her ally Austria, the Prussian invasion was to be condemned, and Maria Theresia would be informed as soon as possible about what her allies would do for her; and: 3) the Republic committed herself to take part in the negotiations with Russia and Saxony, whilst informing France about this resolve, and have her put pressure on Prussia.

Negotiations

The States of Gelderland, Holland, and Overijssel agreed on all three points; Zeeland did not fully agree with condemning Prussia, but awaited further instructions, whilst Utrecht, Groningen, and Friesland were against condemning Prussia, and reluctant to make any promises to Austria before France had been informed about the situation. In order to break this deadlock, Gelderland opted to have the States General write to Utrecht, Groningen, and Friesland, to agree on the matter. When Groningen refused, the States General held a vote, as requested by Holland; with the deputy for Friesland voting in favour – against the wishes of the States of Friesland – the matter was decided with a five-to-two majority.

This did not made matters easier, because although Holland had voted in favour, there was still debate on how to come to Austria's aid. Here, the town councils made themselves heard: Dordrecht opted for sending money only, whilst keeping the French informed; Amsterdam supported Dordrecht and the provinces Utrecht, Groningen, and Friesland in this. It was vital that there would be talks with France about a condemning of the Prussian invasion and how to keep the peace in Europe. The town of Rotterdam was not eager to tell the French everything before any decision was made. Finally, on 25 March – two months after the negotiations with the British – all the towns had reached an agreement and Holland entered her proposal to the States General. By then, France had become suspicious over the long negotiations, and had in the meantime promised Bavaria to send troops to the Holy Roman Empire. If the Republic would send troops to aid Austria, then the war on land would intensify; as a result, France would have less means to fight the British at sea and in the colonies.

The need for a decision became more urgent when the Prussians defeated the Austrians at Mollwitz on April 10. It was no longer possible to delay any answer to Austria. Utrecht and Groningen finally agreed after further negotiations (the States of Utrecht were persuaded by the influential mayor of the Province's capital), whilst the deputy for Friesland again had agreed without consulting the States of Friesland. Accordingly the Republic proclaimed its support of Austria on April 20, whilst condemning the Prussian invasion and demanding a Prussian withdrawal four days later. However, Austria would only receive a subsidy of three million guilders, although it desperately needed troops to withstand the Prussian army. France and Prussia signed the Treaty of Breslau on June 4, in which France would support Charles Albert's claims, with an army of 40,000 men crossing the Rhine to add more pressure, and another one of 40,000 men marching into Westphalia to intimidate the Sea Powers. In July, the Austrians urged the States General to send troops as promised. By then, Britain had already come to the conclusion that there was no other option than to enter the war in Europe and thus promised military support for Austria.

Although France had sent troops into Germany, the Marquis de Fénelon hinted about the Republic and Austrian Netherlands remaining neutral. Utrecht and Groningen thought this was a golden opportunity to stay out of the conflict; Gelderland agreed, but only if the Republic was allowed to at least fulfil her obligations to Austria. Others advocated for troops to be sent to aid Austria. However, the state of the army made it impossible to withstand an attack at that moment: Lieutenant General Isaac Kock baron Cronström (1661–1751), the most senior general officer in the States army and commander of the infantry, had advised not to send more troops to the Barrier towns, in order to avoid weakening the already small field army. If the States garrisons in the Barrier towns had enough provisions, they would be able to hold out any attack, thus compelling the French to attack Austrian garrisons first. The garrison at Mons would be in most danger of an attack, given the poor conditions of the defences and the lack of supplies.

At first it looked as though any French attack along the Meuse could be repelled once plenty of provisions were given to the fortresses of Maastricht, Stevensweert, and Venlo; also, there were enough possibilities to send supplies to Grave, Bois-le-Duc, Breda and Bergen-op-Zoom, so a small field army of 12 battalions and 42 squadrons would suffice to strengthen any garrison along the defensive line when needed. However, with the French in Westphalia, and with Prussia, the Palatine, and Münster posing possible threats, the eastern border was now in serious danger. Cronström therefore advised upon a third augmentation of 20,000 men, and to wait until the next year to gather a field army.

Neutrality

It had already been heard in September 1741, but the ambassador Fénelon made it official in October: George II had as Elector of Hannover negotiated a neutrality convention for Hannover behind the backs of the Republic and Austria. At the same time, he had in his role as King of Great Britain urged the Republic to enter the war over and over again. It was now clear that with this treaty, any military support to Austria became impossible: those willing to enter the war, such as the mayors of Amsterdam, would not want to send troops to do Britain's dirty work. The neutralist and pro-French factions saw this opportunity to enter negotiations with France in order to keep the peace. Austria had to be persuaded to give up some of its territories.

There was again much debate between the provinces: the States of Gelderland, Utrecht, and Groningen opted for neutrality, the States of Holland opposed it because it did not want to see France gaining more power. The town of Amsterdam opposed the neutrality, but regarded an increase of the army with 20,000 men as a provocation; rather, they opted for stressing the friendship between France and the Republic. They even went so far as to send a delegation to the French ambassador to hear what he had to say about the possible neutrality. Therefore, the States General sent a message to France in December to say that they wanted to avoid a war if possible. By January 1742 France had sent an answer: Louis XV would always keep the peace, unless of course he was 'forced' to change his mind. After this rather disappointing answer, Friesland and Overijssel were won over, so now five provinces were in favour of opening negotiations with France about the Republic remaining neutral.

Those who opposed a treaty with France referred to the previous defensive treaty signed in 1717; a new treaty was therefore not needed, so why alienate Britain and Austria? Also, if the Republic wanted to play an important role in Europe, it needed a strong army. By playing out Amsterdam against the States of Holland, there was more time to try and persuade Amsterdam and Dordrecht to agree with the augmentation and keep Holland from deciding on opening negotiations. The safety of the Republic depended on the equilibrium of power in Europe. With George II saying one thing as king but doing another as elector, Austria fighting off Prussian and Franco-Bavarian troops, and a possible French threat coming from the east, the Republic could no longer do nothing and wait for a positive outcome.

1742 started off badly for Maria Theresia, with Charles Albert being elected as Emperor, Frederick II invading Moravia, and a palace revolution in Russia that ended all hope of Russia coming to her aid. At least the British were still motivated to continue the war. Meanwhile, many a heated debate followed in the States of Holland about the third augmentation. Along with the army being increased with 20,000 men, petitions were entered about the building and equipage of 25 new warships, strengthening the fortifications at a cost of one million guilders, and spending a million guilders on the build-up of munitions and supplies for the army. Amsterdam would agree with the augmentation, if the other petitions were agreed upon as well, and if the Austrian Netherlands and Luxembourg should remain neutral ground in any upcoming conflict. A further condition was that Prince Willem IV would not be appointed general in the States Army. These demands made it impossible to reach a conclusion. It did however became clear to everyone that the military situation was dire, and any opposition to the third augmentation and equipping the fleet had to be eradicated. Dordrecht, which firmly chose for neutrality, was put under more and more pressure to give in.

Whilst town councils, provincial states and the States General debated on neutrality, a poem radically influenced public opinion. The writer Willem van Haren published his 'Leonidas', a rather creative translation of Book VII of the *Historiae* by Herodotus about the Persian invasion of Greece in 480 BC. In this, when most Greek states are only willing to protect the Isthmus (the Barrier) and the Peloponnesus (the Republic), the Spartan king Leonidas urges that they come to the aid of Athens (Austria). In translation:

> What speakest thou of Treaty! Thou art Barbarians alike,
> And, like them, at the ready yet
> To break, what was forged so strong
> With Pallas' town, now under threat.
> When that frontier falls, who'll come to Sparta's aid?
> When the archenemy on our land
> Arrives to now overwhelm our armies,
> Who'll offer us a loyal hand?

Easily interpreted as a call for action on behalf of Austria, the poem became an instant success: it was published throughout the Republic, read aloud on the streets and in coffee houses, and gave a voice to the growing frustration among the populace. The people had grown weary of the endless negotiations and the infighting among the Regents. Public support for Austria was strong, as were anti-French sentiments. On February 19, the French ambassador

Fénelon delivered a written statement to the States General, expressing Louis XV's frustration about the hostile attitude in the Republic towards France. Fénelon stressed that it was impossible to withdraw the French troops from Westphalia, since the Republic posed a threat if it decided upon the third augmentation of its army. However, it was of no avail: the Dutch were aware of Fénelon's scheming to delay the States General from reaching a conclusion. Also, news of Austrian successes in February had tipped the scales, and on February 22, the Austrians themselves delivered a letter to the States General, urging the Republic to enter the war on behalf of Austria. Finally, Amsterdam and Dordrecht gave in to the pressure and agreed with the third augmentation.

Mobilisation

All the while, Britain had been more active in supporting Austria. In April, a new subsidy was approved, and General John Dalrymple, Earl of Stair (1673–1747), was sent to The Hague prepare the arrival of 16,000 troops in the Austrian Netherlands, and to revive the defensive alliance between the Republic, Hannover and Britain. Stair, an able commander but lacking any skills regarding diplomacy, managed to alienate the Dutch in a matter of days by bluntly stating British troops would occupy the ports of Oostende and Nieuwpoort – much to the dismay of Amsterdam for obvious reasons – and by talking of big plans for an invasion of France whilst trivialising the possible French threat. Another unexpected visitor was Leopold Philippe Charles Joseph, Duke of Arenberg (1690–1754), commander in chief of the Austrian forces. He boldly claimed there were 24,000 Austrian troops at the ready in the Austrian Netherlands. Together Stair and Arenberg actively tried to persuade the States General to organise a force of 30,000 troops and gather all Allied forces at Tournai. They presented an invasion of France as if it would be like a walk in the park.

The States General, the States of Holland, and the council of Amsterdam were not amused. So despite Stair's protests, the British troops were not garrisoned in Oostende and Nieuwpoort. However, it was now clear that a field army had to be organised soon, before the British changed their mind. A plan was drawn up for the organisation of a field army of 30,000 men. All the provinces agreed, but the possible appointment of the Prince of Orange to the rank of general however proved another hindrance. Holland offered to make Prince Willem IV a lieutenant general, which meant he would be surpassed in rank and seniority by at least 30 other generals; however, Gelderland, Utrecht, Friesland, and Groningen planned to force the matter and offer the rank of general, thereby making him de facto commander-in-chief. All this was of no importance, as news arrived of the peace between Prussia and Austria, signed at Breslau on June 11: Austria had given up Silesia, and in return the Prussian forces were recalled. France had to send her troops from Westphalia and Bavaria in order to relieve the now besieged troops in Prague. Fénelon complained to the States General about the public celebrations that had spontaneously erupted in The Hague, which he was forced to endure. He quickly tried to persuade the Dutch that the troops in Westphalia would not pose a threat, and that the Austrian Netherlands would be safe. However, knowing the French were now in trouble, the decision was made to organise a force of 30 battalions and 50 cavalry squadrons. The French troops in Westphalia had to be pinned down to prevent an advance on the Austrians, who undoubtedly would be overwhelmed, and if needed, an invasion from the Austrian Netherlands into France could commence, with Dutch troops supporting the Austro-British invasion force. On September 19, 12 generals (of whom six were foreign), 18 lieutenant generals – including Prince Willem IV, 30 major generals and 23 brigadiers were appointed. Three days later, the commanding generals Cronström and Willem Maurits, Count of Nassau-Ouwerkerk (1679–1753) took the oath; Crönstrom, already 81 years old at that time, said that 'although he had not heard everything, he would comply with it all.' The commander-in-chief was Lieutenant General Phillip Willem, Baron van der Duyn (1687–1756).

By October, British reinforcements and Hessian and Hanoverian troops had arrived, bringing the total to 42,000 troops under Stair's command. Arenberg added 16,000 Austrians to that, and it was now up to the Republic to send over 30,000 troops

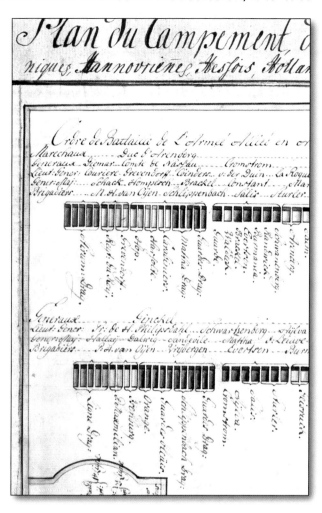

as well. Dordrecht was the only town still vehemently opposed to the idea. By now, the season for campaigning was over anyway. In the end, it was decided by the States General that for the rest of the year a subsidy for Austria would suffice, but that next year an army of 20,000 men was to be organised. But now it was the Province of Utrecht that had objections: the States of Utrecht – led by the deputy Gijsbert Franco, Baron de Milan Visconti (1693–1773) – reasoned that these 20,000 troops would only be the beginning and that it would lead to a war that would drag on for years.

However, during the first months of 1743, the tables seemed to have turned: Prussia had left his allies to fend for themselves; the French troops that had already left Westphalia in August, were halted in their tracks by Austrian opposition; the French troops in Prague had no option but to surrender, and after a ten day march in heavy snow, there was only half of their initial force left. Military support from the Sea Powers would force France to sign a peace with Austria. February and March were spent deliberating on what conditions the army would be put to the field, and if a Stadholder should be reinstated, a touchy subject that only Overijssel supported wholeheartedly. By April, it was clear a decision had to be made, since the British, Hanoverian

Detail from a schematic order of battle of the Pragmatic Army in Germany in 1743. The State infantry and cavalry regiments are listed here, with their uniform colours: all regiments except the Waldeck troops wear blue and red (Anne K.S. Brown Collection)

and Hessian troops would march out back to Germany and the garrisons in the Austrian Netherland would be undermanned. Six battalions and two squadrons were sent to Mons, Ath, and Charleroi, bringing the total of Dutch garrison troops to 20,000 men. Finally in May it was decided that an army of 20,000 men, under the command of generals Cronström and Nassau-Ouwerkerk and consisting of 13 squadrons of cavalry, 11 of dragoons, and 20 battalions of infantry, would be sent (including those already sent to Mons, Ath and Charleroi). Despite ongoing protests and attempt to delay the march by the States of Utrecht, orders were sent to have the army ready.

While further debates dragged on through the summer months, a French army had attacked the Allies as Dettingen on 27 June. The outcome was a victory, albeit not a very decisive one, for the Allies. That same day, the commanders of the Bavarian and Austrian armies met and signed a neutrality pact. In short: several important decisions had already been taken before the Dutch troops would even march into the Holy Roman Empire.

The Army Marches Off
With the last hurdles taken – Nassau-Ouwerkerk was officially appointed commander on 29 July – the army was ready to march off. With 6,000 troops in the Austrian Netherlands, 14,000 troops began the long march towards the Allied army. The route would lead through Münsterland, Paderborn, south through Waldeck to Giessen an der Lahn, and then to Frankfurt am Main. Cronström had advised that the number of men to each battalion to be reduced from 900 to 750, by leaving behind the men that had families: he had observed the English troops a few months before and commented that 'they marched in good order, but I felt more compassion for the women and children of the soldiers'. He therefore thought it wise not to have the troops be followed by a mass of women and children.

However, the baggage train was the least of their worries: desertion was rife, especially among the National regiments. Prussian recruiting officers closely followed the corps and lured away several recruits. This way, each battalion had already lost 100 men, according to Cronström. The bread rations were bad, the long marches across rugged terrain were too much for many recruits, and the number of sick and wounded grew rapidly, so much so that the number of carts for the army were doubled. The troops finally reached the Allied camp near Worms in September. From there on, the combined Allied army marched along the Rhine towards Speyer.

France was alarmed by this move towards its borders and the possible threat to Alsace and Lorraine. Threats were made, which in turn alarmed the Republic that the war might be continued in the Austrian Netherlands the next year. This was confirmed by the British plans to have the 60,000-strong army take up winter quarters there, instead of around Cologne, Liege and Jülich, to which the Austrians, heavily dependent on British subsidies, could only agree. Cronström and Arenberg would have rather gathered the army along the Rhine, in order to attack the eastern border of France the next year. Now, the French were gathering supplies along their northern border, whilst the Allies had none. Of course, the news of the Dutch auxiliary corps being moved to the Austrian Netherlands caused uproar amongst those who had opted for neutrality. To add insult to injury, when the army took up winter quarters on 11 November, the British and Hanoverian troops were given the best quarters in Flanders – close enough to the sea to be evacuated if need be – whilst the Dutch had to make do with the garrison towns Mons, Ath, Charleroi, Courtrai, and Oudenaarde, which were under direct threat of the French forces. By the beginning of 1744, it had become clear that the French were indeed preparing for an invasion.

The Allies, alarmed by the French gathering supplies and artillery, sought a way to take the initiative from the French. The British had drawn up a plan to attack the French first: the first objective of an invasion would be the fortress of Maubeuge; from that point on, Landrecies could be threatened, after which the French line of defence would be broken. This would enable to Austrians to invade the Alsace at the same time. Such was the state and morale of the Allied troops, that their commanders expected an easy victory against the French in battle, should they try to engage the Allied troops. 21,000 British, 16,000 Hanoverian and 6,000 Hessian troops had been sent to the Austrian Netherlands, and provisions were gathered for the offensive to start in April.

The States General however were not so keen on an invasion, since this would lead to an escalation of the conflict, and the Republic would be drawn in even further; as *Raadpensionaris* Anthonie van der Heim (1693–1746) summed up the respective risks taken by Britain and the Republic:

> [T]he former only risking the few men she might actually employ in it, whilst the latter had no sea to skreen (sic) her from undergoing the utmost resentment of an ever covetous & ambitious &, in the case supposed, provoked and victorious neighbour.

The auxiliary corps of 20,000 men would still be available to help the Austrians, and a second corps would be organised soon, but only to defend the Austrian Netherlands and the Holy Roman Empire. Dutch troops could even venture into France if needed, but only in pursuit of French forces, not as part of an invading force. There was good reason not to enter in hostilities with the French. there were 50,000 troops needed for the first line of defence in the Austrian Netherlands, but there were only 32,000 Dutch troops available in the early months of 1744, including the 20,000 strong auxiliary force. Of the 24,000 Austrian troops that Arenberg had boasted about, 7,000 were stationed in Luxembourg. If there were to be no British and Hanoverian troops available to man the garrisons, the States General were not keen on sending more Dutch troops.

On February 19, the Allied commanders discussed how to defend the Austrian Netherlands. The weak spot in the defences was the fortress of Courtrai. The Austrian delegate, Karl Ferdinand Königsegg-Erps (1696 – 1759), said there were indications that the French in all probability would attack Ath and Oudenaarde, in order to split the Allied forces. The Pragmatic Army consisted of 90 infantry battalions and 117 cavalry squadrons. He proposed to have two thirds of the infantry and all the cavalry posted behind the first defensive line, to ensure access to provisions and reinforcements to Courtrai, Oudenaarde, Ath, and Mons.

Meanwhile, the States General and the British panicked over French troops and ships gathering in Dunkerque. The Dutch feared a raid on Holland and the plundering of The Hague, Delft, and other towns. The French however had other plans: Charles Edward Stuart had arrived in Paris, and the French had promised to support his claim to the British crown, with money, arms and troops. The British immediately requested the States General to gather an auxiliary force, as had been done in 1715 and 1719. Six regiments of infantry with artillery support, a total of 6,200 men under command of Lieutenant General Johan Carel Smissaert (1684–1747), were designated to support Britain. De Milan Visconti had opposed sending troops, since he did not believe the Young Pretender to be any threat. When the French fleet was forced to remain in port twice because of a storm, it seemed that he was right. Nevertheless, the French had declared war on Britain on March 15, and the Dutch troops landed in Britain in April, only to return before July.

Charles of Lorraine had been appointed viceroy of the Austrian Netherlands. Cronström called him a man of great capability, others praised his clear vision on military matters and how he seemed to get along easily with everyone. Cronström and Charles agreed on gathering troops between Ath and Mons, since French heavy artillery being gathered at Valenciennes, Cambrai, and Douai indicated an offensive along the rivers Leie or the Scheldt. The fortress of Tournai was deemed too strong for the French to attack, and, it being a Barrier Town, an attack would mean a declaration of war on the Republic. However the new British commander, Field Marshal Wade, decided not to cooperate with this plan, saying he had trouble provisioning his troops. Cronström accused Wade of making up excuses to keep the British force – only 14,000 strong instead of the promised 21,000 – near Oostende, and he was right: with a possible Jacobite invasion in mind, the troops were not to venture off too far. In order to prevent British and Hanoverian troops to be taken prisoner, Wade was under instructions by George II not to have any troops sent into garrisons. To make matters worse, the formation of a German League by Frederick II of Prussia and Charles VII, aiming to halt the Austrian expansion and retake Bavaria, meant that 6,000 Hessian troops were kept in Germany by their Prince and George II had his 6,000 Hanoverian troops sent back. A gathering of Allied troops between Ath and Mons was now impossible. The States General, having heard of this, were therefore not amused when George II also demanded that in accordance with the 1678 treaty, the Republic would declare war on France, in a reaction to the declaration of war by France on Austria on April 23.

The French had considerably more infantry at their disposal since their fortresses and citadels were manned by militia units, but the Allies had more cavalry in the field. Cronström therefore urged his colleagues to take to the field and attack before the French could make their move. Arenberg and Prince Charles agreed, but Wade refused, saying he did not have the means and provisions to have the British troops march south. He was however pressured when Prince Charles offered provisions from the Austrian and Dutch stores. Thus he agreed to have the Allied army gather south of Brussels in May. By then, much time had been wasted and Cronström was furious, fearing the French might take the initiative, whilst the inaction of Wade had resulted in less troops being available for the field army, all garrisons (except Oostende) being manned by Austrian and Dutch troops, and Mons, Menin, and Ypres technically being lost. To make matters worse, Prince Charles announced he would leave Brussels on 7 May and take up command of the Austrian forces in Germany, so the Allies would be without an overall commander.

The Austrian and Dutch commanders tried to persuade Wade to march south, in order to add battalions from the garrisons to the field army, whilst the politicians in The Hague pressured their colleagues in London to instruct Wade to act. With Louis XV joining his troops in Valenciennes on 3 May, a French invasion of the Austrian Netherlands was at hand. The British offered to hire 14,000 Austrian and 16,000 Saxon troops, if the Republic would send an additional 20,000 troops to the Austrian Netherlands. There was still the fear that France might be provoked, and that the Republic again would bear the brunt of the fighting, thus a force of 15,000 men was gathered near Breda instead. A Dutch diplomatic envoy met Louis XV in his headquarters on 16 May. Although Louis said the Republic was to blame for the war in the Austrian Netherlands, the diplomats concluded that the French objective was to tear away the Republic from its allies, particularly since they found out the French soldiers had been ordered not to fight any Dutch troops, but demand they retreat immediately. The following day, when the Dutch envoy still offered to mediate between Austria and France, the French army of 80,000 men with 60 cannon and a massive siege train, invaded the Austrian Netherlands.

The French Invasion Begins

On the first day of the invasion, Colonel the Marquis d'Antin arrived with 800 men at the fortress of Waasten, described by Cronström as being 'an open spot… devoid of any defences'. The commander of the 29-men garrison, Major Terville, refused twice to give up the fortress, but finally retreated to Ypres, in accordance with the advice given earlier to him by Cronström himself. That same day, the French marched into Courtrai, which the Austrians had given up. The loss of this important stronghold led to more tension between the Allied commanders, with Wade being blamed for the dire situation, whilst the States General was urged to send more troops. Nassau-Ouwerkerk and Cronström both pleaded for the 20,000 troops of the second auxiliary corps to be sent, but the States General wanted to send only 12,000 men. Also, the deputies of Friesland, supported by those of Gelderland and Groningen, would only agree if Prince Willem IV was to be made commander of this second corps. After much debate, and the promise to the deputy of Overijssel that his brother would be promoted to brigadier general, the States General voted with a four-to-three majority to send 12,000 men under the command of General Reinhard, Baron Van Reede-Ginkel (1678–1747).

In Britain, Dutch envoys were working alongside British politicians to once again strengthen the ties between Britain and the Republic, which had deteriorated due to British foreign policy in the last years. It led to the British signing a subsidy treaty with Cologne to maintain an army of 10,000 men, to secure the eastern border of the Republic, allowing it to send troops from the garrisons to the field army. The Republic decided to step in as mediator in an attempt to end the hostilities. In its first proposal of July 6 it opted that France end the hostilities in the Austrian Netherlands, acknowledge the Pragmatic Sanction, and send Charles Edward Stuart back to Italy. In return, Austria would give back Bavaria and acknowledge Charles VII as Emperor. As expected, France rejected the proposal: the invasion was a success so far. Nevertheless, the war was only a few months underway, the loss of a few strongholds did not mean the war was lost already, and as a result of the invasion, there was now more unanimity in the States of Holland, and more resolve to work together with the British to force France to her knees once again. Van der Heim expressed his hope the other six provinces would follow suit.

The French had begun to lay siege to Menin on 28 May, declaring France was not at war with the Republic, but wanting to take the fortress from 'the Queen [Maria Theresia] to whom it belonged'. On 1 June, the Allied forces finally crossed the Dender river, in order to take up a strategic position near Oudenaerde, with several large towns nearby, whilst having supplies coming over across the Scheldt. Menin, however, surrendered on 4 June, and the small Dutch garrison under command of Lieutenant General Johan, Baron Van Echteren was given a free passage to Staats-Vlaanderen. Cronström again proposed to meet the French in the field, since their next objective was Ypres. Ypres also was held by a Dutch garrison, commanded by Lieutenant General Wilhelm Ludwig, Prince of Hessen-Phillipsthal. Although an able commander, his force of 3,000 men was not nearly enough to be put up a proper defence. Arenberg did not expect the British forces to advance beyond the line near Deinze, in order to safeguard their lines towards the coast, and therefore rejected the plan to attack.

As expected, Ypres was besieged from 14 June, and fell after only ten days. Again, the Dutch were given free passage to Breda, leaving behind 300 dead and wounded. The Fortress Knokke, defended by 132 men, fell after two days on 29 June; the badly-defended town of Veurne fell after three days on 10 July, with the garrison marching off to Sluis. The fall of one fortress after another urged the States General to send the second corps. By then, the morale among the Allied troops had deteriorated, leading even to Dutch and British soldiers almost fighting each other in Oostende. The British were suspected of negotiating with the French separately, as they had done in 1712, whilst the Austrians were suspected of trying to force the Republic into declaring war on France by their refusal to strengthen the garrisons and fortresses that were manned by Dutch troops. The Republic was blamed in turn for not being clear on its intentions for this campaign. Wade and Arenberg were no longer on speaking terms, and Cronström was caught in the middle.

In July, Prince Charles marched into the Alsace with 60,000 men, which caused the French to send more troops to the east and put a hold on the campaign in Flanders. There would be no attack on Nieuwpoort, Oostende, or Mons, and allied plans were immediately drawn up for a counter offensive. By then, 6,000 more Dutch troops arrived in Oostende, of which two battalions were designated as garrison troops, whilst five battalions would join the main Allied force. All that was needed was a siege train. The States

General argued that Britain and Austria were at war with France, so it was their responsibility. Knowing that neither the British nor the Austrians had the equipment or the personnel for that, the Dutch generals requested the States General to organise one; otherwise, any Allied victory in the field not followed by the taking of fortresses would in the end prove useless. Wade was under pressure to agree with the plans. With the corps of Van Reede-Ginkel added to the field army, the advance began on 6 August towards Tournai, in an attempt to lure the French Marshal Maurice de Saxe from out of his defences behind the Leie river.

The Allied advance into the valley of Lille was spectacular, but chaotic: Allied command had no clear plans on what and where to advance, whilst the rank and file, frustrated over having sat around doing nothing, plundered the countryside. Meanwhile, deputies from the States General had arrived to discuss the plans and costs for the siege of Maubeuge. British siege cannon and equipment were already on their way from Antwerp, and the Republic had to supply everything else, the total cost being 950,000 guilders for a siege of three weeks. The States General decided to send whatever necessary to Brussels, with the costs for transport being paid for by Britain, but kept in mind that there was still no clear plan for the campaign.

With the field army marching aimlessly across the plains around Lille without a siege train, the whole enterprise became a failure. Prussia was again entering the war with an advance through Bohemia, and Prince Charles was recalled from the Alsace. There could be no hope of taking Maubeuge, so there was nothing left but to plunder the French countryside. Cronström offered to take command of a small detachment in the field, in order to get away from the endless bickering at Allied headquarters. He was refused, with the excuse that with Nassau-Ouwerkerk having fallen ill, he would soon have to command the States' forces. Cronström remarked that 'it is a disgrace that nothing has been accomplished with such a great army. Marshal de Saxe said it was an 'Army of Babylon'. By September, there were no more provisions to find around Lille. In order to make the campaign a success, the French army had to be met in the field, and for that, de Saxe and his troops had to be forced to leave their defences. Cronström and Van Reede Ginkel agreed with Arenberg's plan to go around the French defences and lay siege to Courtrai, and after that retake Menin as well. Wade, however, objected to this idea. An alternative plan was to at least have the army take up positions along the river Scarpe, where there were plenty of provisions, and the army foraging the countryside would be a financial blow to the French. It was impossible for Wade to disagree with both plans, and thus the Pragmatic Army marched off to Tournai on 29 September, in order to cross the Scheldt.

Reports came in of French troops nearby, and Cronström and Van Reede-Ginkel immediately called for the army to prepare to engage them. But Wade hesitated; it was agreed to not cross the Scheldt, but send a detachment to surprise the French advance guard at Spiers. The French withdrew and the opportunity to surprise and defeat the French was lost. The army then continued to Oudenaerde. Wade, faced with Cronström, van Reede-Ginkel, and Arenberg united against him and seeing how he inevitably was to be blamed for the failure of the campaign, refused to cross the Leie to attack the French and instead had the army take up positions between Ghent and Brugge. By then, the States General had decided that all Dutch troops, 30,000 in total, were to take up winter quarters in the Austrian Netherlands, mostly in Barrier towns where they had little to fear of a French attack. On 17 October, the British and Hanoverian troops left for their winter quarters in Brussels, Ghent, Oostende, and Brabant. Ironically, the British siege guns were now at Antwerp. The disastrous campaign was over.

It was painfully clear that George II was more interested in preserving his Electorate in Germany than facing the French in the Austrian Netherlands. The Hanoverian troops were recalled to Hannover, for which a request to give the troops a free passage through the Republic was sent. It could of course not be refused, but with the experiences of the last campaign in mind, the Republic demanded that the British would appoint a more suitable commander. If not, then the Republic could no longer be expected to continue supporting a war in which in the end they alone would suffer the consequences. In light of the situation, the third augmentation was to be completed quickly and a fourth augmentation of 12,000 troops planned for next year.

3

The Republic at War, 1745–1746

New Commanders

In 1744, the largest contingent of the Pragmatic Army in the Austrian Netherlands was made up by the Dutch, with a total of 50,000 men in either garrisons, Barrier towns, or in the field. However, unlike during the War of the Spanish Succession, the Republic had no interest in an offensive war against France; her main interest was the defence of the Austrian Netherlands, the Barrier that kept the French away from the Republic's southern borders. France on the other side was also not eager to have to fight both Sea Powers, although Maurice de Saxe welcomed the idea, since the Republic only benefited from its neutrality. France had a good reason to end the war when her protégé Charles VII suddenly died on 20 January 1745. With the Republic still not at war with France, it was believed she could act as mediator between France, Britain, and Austria, and help bring the war to an end.

Cronström announced that he wanted to resign: he was, as he said, too old to command troops in the field. Cronström was right: he was already 83 years old, turning deaf, and was not in the best physical condition. But above all, he was furious and frustrated about the lack of cooperation from Wade during the last campaign. Since there were hardly any suitable commanders to take his place (Nassau-Ouwerkerk and Van Reede-Ginkel – the latter being reluctantly appointed as commander of the cavalry – were not regarded as being capable enough), Cronström's request was therefore denied and he kept his position as commander of the infantry. For the position of commander-in-chief, the States of Overijssel, Gelderland, and especially Friesland were eager to have their Stadholder Prince Willem IV appointed to that position, something that was completely unacceptable to Amsterdam and several other towns. Although Van der Heim assured that the Prince would not be appointed commander in-chief, since this would require a unanimous vote in the States General, he admitted that it was no longer possible, or even desirable, to withhold the Prince of Orange from a command. Despite lengthy debate, the position of commander-in-chief for the next campaign was given to Carl August Friedrich, Fürst zu Waldeck-Pyrmont (1704–1763). Overijssel came with a compromise to appoint the Prince as the youngest general, with the condition that he would never be given an independent command. This was in the end agreed upon. The opposition from the Orangist factions had been a nuisance, and it was remarked that the French only benefited from it (it was sarcastically remarked that if they waited any longer, Waldeck would eventually be Marshal of France), and very unwelcome, now that Britain had sent an envoy to improve the relations with the Republic.

Although the Republic wanted peace, the British envoy was bound by the interests of George II to first and foremost protect Hanover, and by the desire of Maria Theresia to have her husband made Holy Roman Emperor. Thus he could do little more than talk about the next campaign. According to Van der Heim, the Republic would expand the army to 90,000 men with the fourth augmentation, of which 60,000 would constitute the field army (a main force of 46,000 men. with a reserve of 5,000, and 9,000 sent to the Lower Rhine under the command of General Smissaert). In addition, a siege train consisting of 25 24-pounder cannon would be organized. There was much debate about the costs of the next campaign. The Republic felt the financial burden of the war, and was not willing – and not able – to pay more than one quarter of the subsidies. It was finally agreed that Britain would pay three quarters of the costs, provided that all the siege equipment would be delivered by the Republic, and pay one third of the total costs for the artillery and sieges. Also on the agenda was the appointment of an overall commander of the Allied forces. Wade was, of course, unacceptable. Prince Charles was unfortunately unavailable, so Maria Theresia suggested Field Marshall Lothar Joseph, Count Königsegg-Rothenfels (1673–1751), an able and experienced commander (who was also the Austrian envoy in the negotiations at Antwerp on the Barrier Treaty in 1714–1715). Britain was reluctant to have her troops fighting under a 'foreign' commander. As a compromise, Prince William Augustus, Duke of Cumberland (1721–1765), would be sent to formally take command, although Königsegg-Rothenfels would be the actual commander.

The upcoming campaign would certainly involve a French siege of Tournai, from whence the Allied forces had invaded the plains of Lille the previous year, and, as Cronström expected, the French would not sit around and wait for the Allies to bring a siege train this time. After taking Tournai, the French could then advance along the Scheldt to Oudenaarde, and would pose a threat to Flanders and Brabant. The Mons to Tournai road would therefore have to be occupied by an Allied force, keeping the French at bay and also within reach of Maubeuge, Condé, Valenciennes, and Le Quesnoy. This meant the British had to set up magazines in the aforementioned towns. Cronström however feared that, with part of the Austrian and Hanoverian troops gone, there would be little else to do but once again gather an army near Brussels and wait for the next French move. The States Géneral sent out 18 more battalions to complete the promised number of 41 battalions for the field army; Waldeck arrived in Brussels in April to take command of the Pragmatic Army.

Königsegg-Rothenfels proposed to gather the Allied army near Halle, from where Brussels, Ath, and Mons would be covered. It was however too far from Tournai to prevent the town being besieged by the French. There were only 40,000 troops available, and the newly arrived British commander, the Duke of Cumberland, was not yet familiar with the whole situation. Van

Reede-Ginkel, commanding the Dutch cavalry and also quartermaster-general, was absent, which added to the difficulties. This made it impossible to anticipate the French plans or react quickly to any French move. This became clear when French forces arrived at Mons and Malplaquet on 22 April: it proved to be a diversion, because three days later, the French began their siege of Tournai. Waldeck could not believe the French would attempt to capture the town, since it had a garrison of 8,000 men, with plenty of cannon, ammunition and provisions, and commanded by the 84-year-old veteran General Johan Adolf, Baron van Dorth (1661–1747), an elderly yet capable commander. Yet on 1 May, the French opened the siege lines towards the town, just as Cronström had predicted.

Although the town was sufficiently provided with men and provisions, and the citadel regarded as near impregnable, the outer defence works were not kept in good condition, which was a hindrance to the defenders. This had a bad effect of the moral of the men. On 7 May, the powder magazine in the citadel exploded, which cost many lives. Nevertheless, the Dutch put up a staunch defence, attacking the siege lines five times. The Allied commanders decided it was time to break up camp and meet the French in the field. On 2 May, the Allied army advanced against Tournai, arriving 10 km south west of the town on the 9th.

The Battle of Fontenoy

Upon arrival, the Allied command learned that the French army had taken up defensive positions near Fontenoy, with a series of redoubts in their front. Cronström was more experienced in war in Western Europe than Waldeck: the latter had fought in the War of the Polish Succession and the Austro-Turkish War (1737–1739), conflicts that were fought with highly mobile armies fighting in vast open terrain, unlike the wars in the more densely populated Austrian Netherlands. He advised to take up positions in the vicinity and threaten the French. Waldeck however was eager for action, as was the inexperienced Cumberland; they both urged Königsegg-Rothenfells to attack. On 10 May, British troops chased away a French outpost in the village of Vezon, whilst Dutch troops occupied the village of Bourgeon; the Allies then set up their army along the line Vezon – Bourgeon – Peronne. It was decided that the Allied forces would attack the next morning.

The plan that was devised focused on the area between the villages of Fontenoy and the Barry woods: the Dutch contingent, along with Hanoverian and Austrian troops, was given the task of attacking the French positions in Fontenoy and Antoing; Brigadier General Ingoldsby would attack the Barry woods with four regiments, to secure that flank when Lieutenant General Ligonier would lead the massed infantry attack in the centre. It was a bold idea, but it relied heavily on the success of the attacks on the flanks. A reconnaissance in the early hours of the 11th led to the discovery of a French redoubt near the Barry woods, which meant that the flank attack there would meet some fierce resistance.

At 2:00 am, the Allied army, about 46- to 48,000 strong, took up positions, and opened the battle with a long range artillery barrage from about 40–50 cannon. Unfortunately, since these were all three- and six-pounder guns,

Ambitious France and haughty Spain
Unite the Horns of Pow'r to gain;
Against them England drags the Tail;
While the sly Dutchman fills his Pail.

THE BENEFIT
of
NEUTRALITY

Thus oft Contention haps to rise
Between two Dogs, a Bone the Prize;
A neutral Cur, who sees the Fray,
Steals in and bears the Bone away.

Publish'd Dec. 26. 1745. according   to Act of Parliament by C Goodwin. Pr. 6.ᵈ

'The Benefits of Neutrality', a British cartoon published in 1745 about the War of the Austrian Succession: France, Britain and Spain fight over a cow, whilst the Dutchman is milking it. Published by C. Goodwin. (Rijksmuseum)

the bombardment had very little effect on the enemy positions in the woods and the redoubts. Waldeck had moved his forces more forward during the night, and lined up the infantry immediately the next morning, 12 battalions facing Fontenoy, with four cavalry squadrons in support, eight battalions in the centre towards the redoubts between Fontenoy and Antoing, and 36 squadrons of cavalry in support on his left. Added to the infantry were three batteries of artillery. Waldeck was however not aware of the strength of the French positions: Fontenoy was heavily fortified, and the troops there had suffered little to no damage from the artillery barrage. Waldeck had positioned his troops early in the morning and eagerly requested to advance against Fontenoy; he was given the order shortly after 9:00 am, when the British and Hanoverian troops had finished taking up their positions. The French defences at the entrance to the village were easily swept aside, but it was at the cemetery, surrounded by a wall six foot high and reinforced with a ditch and palisades, that the Dutch attack was met with a murderous fire, and forced to retreat. The attack by the Anglo-Hanoverian column was repulsed similarly. Reinforced by Austrian cavalry and two British battalions, the Allied troops advanced a second time; despite the conduct of the Dutch Guards and three Swiss regiments, the other battalions fled, and this attack

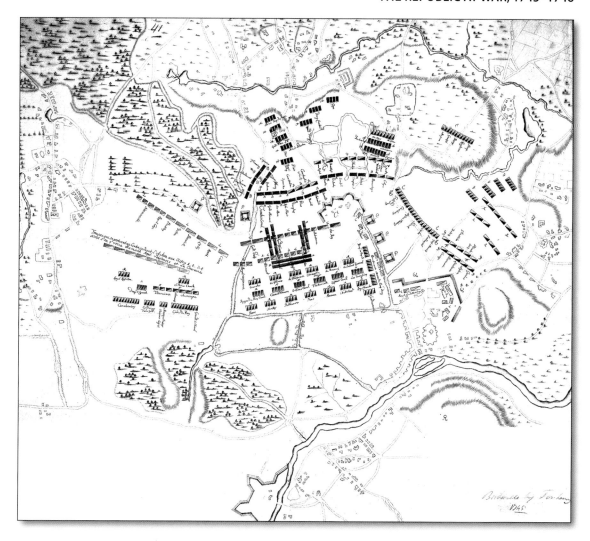

The Battle of Fontenoy, plan in pen and watercolour by an anonymous artist, 1745. (Rijksmuseum)

was also repulsed with heavy losses. Meanwhile, Cronström led his eight battalions against Antoing, but being under heavy fire from the redoubts and from French artillery on the left of the Scheldt, the column faltered before it reached Antoing at all. The cavalry could do little but turn around and take up a position to the rear, covering the retreat of the infantry. The Hesse-Homburg regiment, commanded by Colonel Appius, turned and fled after the first volley, and would not stop until they reached Ath, where Appius wrote the Council of State that 'all was lost'.

Meanwhile, the British and Hanoverian battalions under Ligonier, forming one massive column, pressed on their attack. Cumberland, against the advice of Waldeck and Königsegg-Rothenfells, placed himself at the head of the column, as it tore through the French line and was on the verge of breaking through. But Ingoldsby had hesitated to attack the French positions in his sector, thus leaving also the other flank unprotected. Desperately, de Saxe had wave after wave of French cavalry charge the redcoats, until his infantry had reorganized. Now under fire from three sides, the British column slowly ground to a halt. The momentum was lost and the army retreated, leaving behind 7,500 dead and wounded. The Dutch lost about 1,200 men.

Morale among the Allied commanders was low. The British command was eager to blame Waldeck for the attack, saying he had promised an easy victory. Cumberland and Königsegg-Rothenfels openly questioned the bravery and skills of the Dutch troops, the former calling them 'great scoundrels' who were only fit for garrison duties. But it was clear that Cumberland had made some grave mistakes, by agreeing with and leading the attack on the plains between Fontenoy and the Barry woods, without having properly gathered information on the strength and position of the enemy. All in all, most Dutch troops – especially the cavalry – had performed rather well, and shown they did not lack bravery, having held their positions under heavy fire. Thus the States General answered the insult, stating that they:

> [H]ad wished that her troops could have fulfilled all the expectations of his lordship the field marshal, but that after more than thirty years of peace, it is no small wonder when all the troops were brought for the first time under the eye of an enemy, they do not act with the same vigour and grimness, especially when they are exposed for several hours to a strong and uncommon fire, and having to be led, not in the open field, but against a superior and favourably positioned enemy.

Cronström was a veteran from the battle of Malplaquet (11 September 1709), where Dutch troops successfully attacked the French right wing, advancing steadily through a hail of bullets, and driving the French back, despite heavy losses. He commented:

> There have been some of our troops that have performed badly. There have been few who have fled from a cannon-shot. It must not be believed, sir, that these troops are like those from the past war.

Waldeck laid the blame with the officers and he complained to the States General about their lack of bravery: 'They obey even less on a day of combat than on other occasions.' Nevertheless, he advised to only punish those who had been accused of cowardice, instead of persecuting every officer who had neglected his duty, since this would 'harm the reputation of the States army even more, and bring shame to many families at home'. Colonel Appius and others were made into an example and dishonourably discharged.

Their victory at Fontenoy opened up new possibilities for the French to make peace proposals to the Republic. Maybe, the Republic could be persuaded to sign a separate peace with France, as had the British done in 1712. But the States General had already offered a peace proposal the year before, and stated it was France's turn to come up with a new proposal. Also, there could be no negotiations without Britain involved, although there were some who would not hesitate to sign a separate peace with France if Britain refused to agree with reasonable terms. A proposal to hold a peace conference in The Hague with all parties involved was welcomed by the Republic and France, but there was no agreement on what should be discussed and what the terms of peace would be. Furthermore, a peace congress could only come to pass if there was a ceasefire in the Austrian Netherlands. The French were rather disappointed about the reaction of the States General. Furthermore, a ceasefire was out of the question, since France's military successes gave her a strong position at the negotiations. Indeed, the campaign, and the string of successes, were not over by far.

The Fall of Tournai

The defeat at Fontenoy meant the siege of Tournai continued. After three weeks of hard fighting, the French had finally breached the main wall, and the commander Van Dorth offered to have part of the garrison retreat into the citadel and surrender the town. De Saxe however demanded he surrender the town and the citadel, or else he should retreat into the citadel with the entire garrison plus the women and children, a total of 8,200 people in a citadel that had room for 2,500 at most. Van Dorth asked if he could send an officer to The Hague for further instructions. This was refused, but de Saxe hinted that, if he would surrender the town immediately, the women and children, as well as the sick and wounded, could remain in the town. Van Dorth agreed, and the French entered Tournai on 24 May. Two officers arrived in The Hague two days later. They were sent back with two instructions: to either surrender the citadel under the most favourable terms, or to stand and fight as long as possible. It was left to Königsegg-Rothenfels to decide which one Van Dorth would receive.

Both orders arrived on the 30th and were discussed by the Allied commanders. Cumberland was furious, demanded the citadel would be defended to the last man, and cursed the surrender of the town. Cronström was the only one who gave a rebuttal, saying that if there was hope the citadel could hold out for six more weeks, than they had to continue the defence, but that the reality was that there were only enough provisions for a mere three weeks. It would be wise to save the garrison, since its eleven battalions would be a welcome reinforcement to the field army. Königsegg-Rothenfels, pressured by Cumberland, decided to send the second order to Van Dorth, saying the garrison could do great damage to the besiegers. Added to the order was the strict stipulation that the women and children would have to be left outside the citadel. The French, he explained, were no barbarians and would certainly look after them. The next day, the orders were handed to Major General Van Brakel, the second-in-command; Van Dorth had suffered a stroke, and was allowed by de Saxe to leave the town with full military honours.

The French, who had used the eight-day ceasefire to bring their artillery into position, started bombarding the citadel on 1 June. The overcrowded citadel, where the men had built shelters in every possible place, was pounded relentlessly. Still, the garrison undertook several counterattacks, and French losses were mounting. De Saxe, in an attempt to break the defenders morale, refused to allow the inhabitants of Tournai to give shelter the women and children, who were forced to roam the streets and sleep in the open air, and had the baggage that was left behind by the officers plundered. Louis XV finally took pity in the women and children and allowed them to be transported to Oudenaerde.

After 18 days of relentless bombardments by 200 heavy guns and 78 mortars, the citadel had been pounded to ruins, and the main wall breached. Van Brakel invited the French to negotiate the terms of surrender. The garrison would be allowed free passage to Ghent, if they would not be deployed against the French, nor be placed in garrisons in the Austrian Netherlands, until 1 January 1747. This meant the remaining 6,000 men could not be used for 18 months, save for garrison duty in the Republic itself. Cumberland despised the surrender: the surrender of the citadel was proof of 'Dutch politicks' and of 'the inexpressible cowardice of their generals and troops'. The French, however, seeing the immense destruction that their bombardments had caused, and the horrible circumstances under which the Dutch troops had performed their duties, praised the Dutch and their commander; as expressed in the words of the French Minister of Foreign Affairs d'Argenson: 'We owe justice to Mr. Brakel to say that he made a fine defence of the citadel of Tournai'.

Since Cumberland refused to have British troops perform garrison duties, more Dutch battalions were taken out of the field army. The Pragmatic Army was now 40,000 strong, but de Saxe had 100,000 troops under his command. He sent part of his force to Ath, which caused the Allies to retreat. His diversion had worked, and the main army then marched towards Oudenaarde. The Austrian Lieutenant General Moltke was sent to Ghent with 5,000 men in order to strengthen the garrison, but was defeated on 9 July near Melle. Moltke retreated towards Ghent with 1,000 men, while the rest retreated towards Aalst, leaving behind 700 dead and wounded, as well as 1,400 prisoners. Now, the Allies were in a predicament: they had to either give up Flanders or Brabant. On July 11, a French force under Lieutenant General Count Löwendahl made a surprise attack on Ghent, capturing the town after little resistance. While the British contingent fled towards the citadel, Moltke escaped with his remaining 400 cavalry towards Sluis; the governor of Sluis, Lieutenant General Johan Dibbets, refused to let Moltke and his men take refuge there, having had the explicit orders not to give access to any troops without a letter of consent of the States General. This embarrassing incident led to the States General immediately issuing a resolution that all Allied troops were to be given access to fortresses and garrisons under Dutch command.

On 15 July, the British troops in the Ghent citadel surrendered. 3,000 troops and a vast amount of military provisions fell into French hands. The loss of Ghent led to the quick capture of Bruges on the 18th and Oudenaarde on the 21st; de Saxe went on to capture Dendermonde on 13 August, a town whose defences were even more neglected. An attempt to send reinforcements failed. Oostende, already under siege from 7 August, capitulated on 23 August after a half-hearted defence. With the capture of Nieuwpoort on 5 September, de Saxe had captured the whole of Flanders; to secure his position, he captured Ath on 9 October, the loss of which was another disappointment for the Dutch, since Antwerp and Brussels were now under threat. The Dutch garrisons of Dendermonde and Oostende were allowed to march out under the same conditions as the garrison of Tournai, meaning more troops would not be available for the field army in the next campaign.

The Republic Betrayed

In September, the French played out another card: Charles Edward Stuart, the 'Young Pretender', had landed in Scotland, proclaimed his father King, and marched at the head of a small army towards Edinburgh. As expected, the British withdrew a large part of their army from the Netherlands. Despite the shortage of troops, the Republic sent once again an expeditionary force of 6,000 men to help quell the rebellion. This force was composed of the garrison forces from Tournai and Dendermonde – sending them to Britain was a loophole in the agreement that the States General gladly exploited. Without the British contingent, the Dutch had to use all their available troops, 80,000 in total, to man the Barrier towns and safeguard their borders. Waldeck did his utmost to prepare the defences of Brussels, having 66 battalions and 97 squadrons under his command (of which 39 battalions and 46 squadrons were Dutch), against de Saxe's army of 126 battalions and 164 squadrons. The rapid French advance towards Staats-Vlaanderen had caused panic; but the States General were assured that no French troops would cross the borders of the Republic: Louis XV had previously sent requests to the governors of the garrisons and fortresses in Staats-Vlaanderen to have markers placed where the border was, so as not to have French troops cross the border by mistake: 'The King is firmly resolved to spare the States-General'. Besides, the destruction of the port of Oostende by the French would be only of benefit to the Republic. By December, all British troops had departed, leaving only 8,000 Hanoverians and 6,000 Hessians in winter quarters, the latter being shipped to Britain immediately after news of a planned French invasion caused more unrest.

It became clear that Britain was unwilling to continue the war in the Austrian Netherlands, since Parliament had opted for withdrawing all troops altogether and continuing the war against France on sea and in the colonies. To them, the Jacobite victory at Prestonpans was of more significance than the possible fall of Antwerp or Brussels. Furthermore, since Austria seemed obsessed with recapturing Silesia and the war in Italy rather than fighting the French, negotiations with France on peace – and perhaps even on neutrality – were necessary and justified. Envoys were sent to Versailles in January and February 1746 to negotiate a separate peace treaty. The French expected that the Republic, under influence of the Amsterdam council and merchants, would want to withdraw from the war, which would then force the British, already under pressure from the threat of Jacobite and French invasions, to agree with peace negotiations. Indeed, there was now little left of the Barrier, and if Brussels, Antwerp and other towns were captured, the border of the Republic itself would be threatened.

To prevent an invasion of the Republic, it was necessary for the Allies to start an offensive. According to Waldeck, a force of 109,000 troops was needed, including 22,000 garrison troops. To gather such a force proved difficult, the Dutch units having lost many men to sickness and desertion; German troops, especially Saxon and Bavarian troops, were unavailable. Austria, afraid the Republic might indeed negotiate a separate peace, finally agreed to send two undermanned corps to the Austrian Netherlands, a total of 20,800 men instead of the promised 39,200; Field Marshal Carl Joseph,

Prince Batthyányi (1697–1772) was appointed commander of the Austrian forces in the Netherlands. There was much frustration about Britain, who, as the representatives for Foreign Affairs remarked, 'seemed to need 50,000 troops to quell a rebellion of no more than 6,000 Jacobites'. The British promised 50,000 men for the next campaign, as long as the Republic would again bring 50,000 men in the field as well, and complete the third and fourth augmentation with German troops. The Allied army would consist of 114,000 men, but alas only on paper.

The Allies were taken by surprise when de Saxe launched an offensive against Brussels with 26,000 men on 29 January, opening siege lines on 7 February. The Brussels garrison consisted of 17 battalions and four squadrons, commanded by Lieutenant General Van der Duyn; there were 18 battalions in the garrisons of Antwerp, Namur, Mons and Charleroi, leaving 19 battalions for a field army to relieve Brussels. The Council of State advised Waldeck to give up on Brussels and withdraw the garrisons of Namur and Mons, to prevent these from being taken prisoner. Waldeck, however, wanted to keep garrisons in Mons and Charleroi, since these were not in danger of being besieged and in order to be able to launch an offensive there to threaten the French border. Brussels would be able to hold out, since the weather was still bad. However, the States General ordered the troops to withdraw, and have the garrisons replaced by Austrian troops, which were expected to arrive on 20 February.

On 9 February, Van der Duyn launched a counterattack on the French siege lines. The attack, in the dark of night and in bad weather, failed. De Saxe sent a message the following day, stating the defense of Brussels was hopeless, and the longer the siege progressed, the more he feared his men might resolve to plunder when the town was inevitably captured. Van der Duyn was not intimidated, and despite the walls being breached on the 16th, he decided to hold out at least until the 20th when Austrian reinforcements would arrive, as promised in a note by Waldeck. After a French attack on the 19th, which the Dutch could barely fight off, it was clear the situation was indeed hopeless. Van der Duyn tried to delay the negotiations as long as possible, but when no reinforcements arrived on the 20th, Brussels was surrendered. The garrison was sent to captivity in France on the 23rd. Despite many men having been on leave during the winter, and hundreds of men having escaped after the surrender, 6,000 of the best troops, including nine Swiss battalions, and all the field artillery, were lost. With support from, among others, Cronström and Van der Duyn, Waldeck chose to strengthen Antwerp with whatever troops he still had available, and posted 25,000 men in a strong position behind the Dijle river, between Mechelen and Aarschot.

De Saxe received a hero's welcome in Paris; he had brought with him, along with several Dutch colours and standards, the standard of Francis I, which was captured by Charles V at the Battle of Pavia in 1525.

The Campaign of 1746

The peace negotiations took months, but in the end, there were no results. One of the greatest hindrances was Britain's unwillingness to give up Cape Breton, the French colony that had been captured by British colonials; it was their only military success so far. For the Republic, the situation increasingly worsened: the French had recalled their diplomats from The Hague, two Barrier towns and several other garrison towns were being dismantled, 12 battalions and three squadrons were not available for the field army after their surrender, whilst 6,000 troops were taken captive and would not be exchanged. The garrisons of Mons, Namur, and Charleroi were regarded as lost.

After the Austrian troops had joined the Pragmatic army in March, Waldeck tried to raise the spirit of the troops with an attack on Vilvoorde, near Brussels, in the early morning of 7 April. Waldeck had shown his bravery, but the attack of which he proudly wrote to the States General led to much criticism and fears that his rash actions would provoke the French to start the campaign season early. By May, de Saxe had gathered his field army near Brussels, numbering around 100,000 men. Waldeck and Batthyányi anticipated an offensive against Antwerp and decided not to await a French attack, knowing the French outnumbered their forces two-to-one. The line along the Dyle was therefore abandoned. On 22 May, the Allied army took up positions behind the lines near Terheijden, between Geertruidenberg and Breda, leaving Antwerp open to the French. Waldeck hoped this would at least buy the Allies some time to gather their forces and start a counter offensive. Indeed, a Hessian and a Hanoverian contingent were on their way; the Austrians sent another corps of 12,000 men, along with the popular Prince Charles of Lorraine to once again take command.

As expected, the French opened their siege lines around Antwerp on 25–26 May, and bombarded the citadel with 9,000 projectiles. By the 31st, the walls had already been breached, and the town surrendered the next day. The French had not decided yet what to do next: an invasion of the territory of the Republic could force the Republic to sue for peace, but they feared it would lead again to a revolution, with the Prince of Orange being appointed Stadholder – as had happened in 1672. If this happened, it was to be expected that to legitimize his appointment Prince Willem IV would not hesitate to step up the war effort far more aggressively, having united the provinces behind him. The campaign would therefore be continued in Flanders against the three remaining frontier towns Mons, Charleroi, and Namur.

The French began their siege of Mons on 24 June. Mons was defended by a garrison of 2,200 Dutch and 1,600 Austrian troops, commanded by Lieutenant General Hessen-Phillipisthal – the same unfortunate commander who surrendered Ypres two years earlier. After a discouraging report from the senior engineer officer, explaining the town could last out perhaps a few more days, negotiations started, and the garrison capitulated on 11 July. The whole garrison was led into captivity, leaving 50 dead and 80 wounded behind.

Waldeck, whose reputation had been tarnished by the capture of Brussels and the retreat to Terheijden, was eager to advance. The army, reinforced by a Hanoverian corps, the Hessians that returned from Britain, and four British battalions, began their advance on 17 July; an Austrian force joined them on the 23rd. Prince Charles of Lorraine took over command from Waldeck and Batthyányi; but he did not show the same energy and vigour as he had done in 1744 when he crossed the Rhine into the Alsace. The French were therefore able to take St. Ghislain on 25 July, a small fortress where a few hundred defenders had held out for almost 60 days; and then Charleroi on 3 August, whose 1,400 defenders were also taken into captivity after a half-hearted defence of a mere five days. Charles decided on taking up positions between the Sambre and the Mehaigne rivers, in an attempt to defend Namur. However, Namur was dependant on provisions coming from Maastricht, and it was feared that once this line was cut off, the army again had to retreat. Indeed, de Saxe sent out Löwendahl with 16 battalions, two dragoon regiments, and some light troops to capture the town of Huy. This he did without any trouble; 80,000 bread provisions were captured. Another force of 1,600 men, raided Liège and captured 32 ships, containing fodder and flour. By August 26, the Pragmatic Army began to feel the loss of these provisions, and despite the well-intended protests by Waldeck, Prince Charles was forced to retreat across the Meuse, leaving Namur to fend for itself. The garrison of Namur was strengthened with eight Dutch battalions and two Austrian battalions (bringing the total to 13 battalions and one squadron, 7,350 men in all), but the men knew full well that this meant they were bound to be taken prisoner. Morale therefore was low.

Thus as the Pragmatic Army had retreated, the siege of Namur began on September 12. As soon as the siege started, the 88-year old General Colyear handed over command to Lieutenant General Crommelin and left town. Already on the 18th, the French almost breached the main wall. Crommelin surrendered the town in order to retreat into the citadel on the 21st and 22nd. During this lull in the fighting, 2,000 men deserted. And even worse, when the French resumed the siege, an ammunition store exploded, after which all the buildings in the citadel burned to the ground. Heavy bombardments started on the 27th, and all seemed lost. Those not wanting to await the inevitable capture, deserted by the dozens. Crommelin offered to capitulate, under the condition that the garrison could march out, but the French would only accept an unconditional surrender. After deliberating with his officers, he surrendered the citadel on 30 September. What was left of the garrison, 3,700 men, was taken prisoner.

The Battle of Rocoux
The Pragmatic Army, having secured their lines of provisions, had crossed the Meuse on 14 September to relieve Namur. But things were not going well at the Allied headquarters: Waldeck was not content with Prince Charles as commander; he was even reprimanded by the States General for failing to show him proper courtesy. The appointment of the Lieutenant General Ligonier (who commanded merely four battalions and nine squadrons of British troops) as second-in-command by Charles was the proverbial final straw: Waldeck took the Dutch troops – 13 battalions and 50 squadrons – and three Austrian battalions, and organised his own independent command. A half-hearted attempt was made to advance towards Namur, but the threat of the French army, followed by the news of the quick surrender of the town, put an end to that. Charles was desperate: his only hope was that the French would meet him in the field.

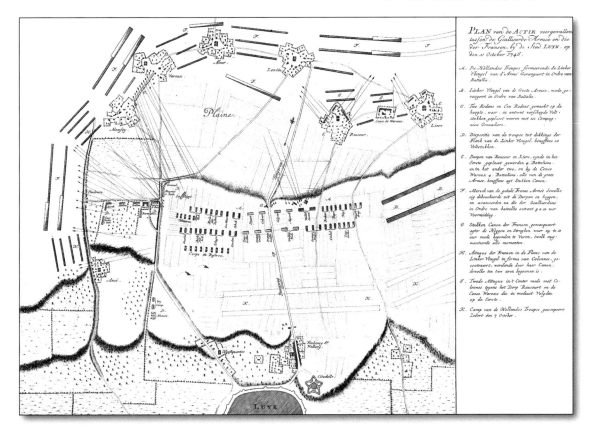

Plan of the battle of Rocoux, showing the positions of the Dutch troops on the left flank. (Rijksmuseum)

With Namur, the last frontier town, captured, de Saxe was willing to oblige: one victory was all he needed to secure the capture of the frontier towns, before he would let his army take up winter quarters. He found the Pragmatic Army near Rocoux, with its back to the Meuse. If there was any chance to finally defeat the Allied armies, it was here. The Allied troops had taken up strong positions, in order to defend Liège and Maastricht. The left wing was taken up by the Dutch; the British, Hanoverian and Hessian troops took up the centre, while the Austrians took up the right wing. In front of the line were several villages that were fortified; between those, redoubts were built. The result was a 'very strong camp, and right so, for if the enemy would break through, the whole army would be thrown into the Meuse', as the States Generals' representative to the Field Army Willem van Haren wrote.

De Saxe, who had about 110,000 men at his disposal against the Allies' 80,000, was in good spirits and on 11 October, directed his main attack against what he perceived was the weakest link: the Dutch troops at the left. But these were not the same troops he had seen at Fontenoy: the old but still very capable infantry commander Cronström had worked tirelessly on improving the infantry battalions under his command. Despite the many losses of the last year, the Dutch had not lost heart. The French began with a counter-battery fire against the Dutch artillery position near the village Ans, which had wreaked havoc on the French columns for about two hours, followed by an advance of 20 battalions towards the Dutch lines. After hard fighting, the French captured Ans. With the arrival of reinforcements under General

Smissaert, an attempt was made to recapture the village, but the Dutch were driven back. They took up a new position under cover of the cavalry, but when Waldeck heard of the capture of Rocoux by the French, he decided to retreat towards the centre, where the British, Hanoverians and Hessians also stood their ground. The Austrians however, had not fired a shot: Charles wanted to keep the road to Maastricht secure and would not send troops to support the faltering lines. Before the sun was down, the Pragmatic Army had retreated towards the St. Pietersberg, under the cover of the cannon of Maastricht.

The Dutch had lost 1,768 men, two pairs of colours and several cannon. The French losses were twice those of the Allies; among the fallen was the former ambassador Fénelon. Waldeck wrote to the States General: 'The troops have fought with such goodwill, bravery and steadfastness, that they have redeemed the Netherlands' name and fame of old'. 'The Dutch behaved incomparably well,' wrote Leveson Gower to the Duke of Bedford, 'insomuch that they lost many of their officers, and some of their best regiments are almost ruined'. Waldeck was again blamed for the defeat, and was said to '[treat] this affair in his account as a thing of no great consequence', calling it 'the action near Liège' instead of a battle. Nevertheless, Rocoux took away the shame about the surrender of Charleroi and Namur, and improved the reputation of the Dutch infantry. It was time to take up winter quarters.

(This history of the army and its campaigns will be continued in the second part of this work; for the remainder of this volume we now turn to the military organisation of the Republic, and the details of its infantry.)

4

Infantry Structure and Organisation

The Dutch Republic wielded a formidable force in wartime. However, as soon as the hostilities were over, the numbers were again reduced. A standing army, although useful, was a costly affair. Of the many regiments raised, only a small number remained in permanent service: in the *Rampjaar* 1672 for instance, 30 infantry regiments were taken into service. Only six of these remained when, two years later, there was no more imminent danger and the army was again reduced; and over time, three more were either disbanded or amalgamated. Since the population of the Republic was not large enough to find enough recruits, the National Infantry Regiments ('*Regimenten Nationalen*') also recruited abroad, especially in the Austrian Netherlands and Germany, although recruiting in some German states was prohibited. In all, 40 to 60 percent of the rank and file were foreign. Some of the National regiments were raised as foreign regiments, but had been nationalised over the years. This happened last in 1783 when the three Scottish regiments of the Scots Brigade were taken into the line as National Regiments 22, 23, and 24. Shortly before the death of Prince Willem III in 1702, the infantry consisted of the following:

Infantry Regiments	62,243
Subsidy troops:	
Brandenburg	1,680
Mecklenburg	1,680
Hannover	4,452
Hesse-Kassel	2,460
Electoral Palatinate	3,168
Denmark	3,222
Total:	16,662
Total for the infantry:	78,905 officers and men

As mentioned earlier, Holland, being the largest and richest province, paid for most of these troops; it had 19 national regiments on its establishment, as well as the bulk of the foreign regiments. Friesland had seven regiments,

Utrecht five, Zeeland four, Groningen and Gelderland each three, Overijssel two. Drenthe had one regiment, consisting of one battalion.

With the War of Spanish Succession raging on, more troops were hired. In 1710, the infantry numbered:

Infantry Regiments	77,300
Subsidy troops:	
Brandenburg	1,680
Mecklenburg	1,680
Hannover	4,452
Hesse-Kassel	2,240
Electoral Palatinate	6,193
Denmark	4,000
Munster	1,600
Prussia	2,217
Württemberg	1,700
Saxony	3,300
Brunswick	1,400
Holstein	797
Total:	31,169
Total for the infantry:	108,469 officers and men.

In 1718, the peacetime strength was set on 34,148 officers and men, including 2,000 Swiss troops that were paid for from the Barrier subsidies. This was barely enough to man the Barrier and the garrisons, leaving no troops for a field army. And since this was the paper strength, the effective number of officers and men was even lower, numbering around 29,000.

In the years to follow, the army was again either increased or decreased, depending on the situation:

	Paper strength	Effective strength	
1727	54,316	50,000	
1736	44,486	40,000	
1741	65,060	60,000	(after the first and second augmentations)
1743	84,748	70,000	
1744	84,748	80,000	(after the third augmentation)
1745	96,748	85,000	(after the fourth augmentation)
1747	96,784	65,000	
1748	126,748	90,000	(after the fifth augmentation)
1753	38,000	33,000	

Every augmentation took months, if not years, to be completed. The effective strength was of course in the 1740s influenced by the war: for instance, during 1746, 12,000 men had been taken prisoner. By the end of that year, the fourth augmentation could only be completed by hiring six Bavarian battalions. When Prince Willem IV was elected Stadholder, and given the rank of captain-general by all the provinces, a fifth augmentation of 30,000 men was ordered, plus the hiring of 15,000 Russian troops. Once the war was over, the army was again greatly reduced: several regiments

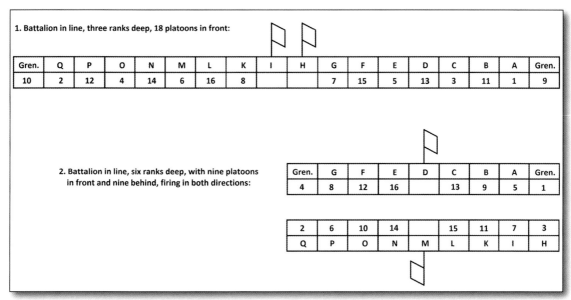

1. Battalion in line, three ranks deep, 18 platoons in front:

Gren.	Q	P	O	N	M	L	K	I	H	G	F	E	D	C	B	A	Gren.
10	2	12	4	14	6	16	8			7	15	5	13	3	11	1	9

2. Battalion in line, six ranks deep, with nine platoons in front and nine behind, firing in both directions:

Gren.	G	F	E	D	C	B	A	Gren.
4	8	12	16		13	9	5	1

2	6	10	14		15	11	7	3
Q	P	O	N	M	L	K	I	H

Schematic representation of platoon firing by a battalion, based on a sketch from the 1720s: the musketeer companies were divided into 16 platoons, and each platoon given a letter A–Q. Platoons A–G formed the right side of the line, platoons K–Q the left side; platoons H and I were the colour parties, which were kept in reserve in the centre, whilst the grenadiers (Gren). were grouped on either flank. All platoons, including the grenadiers, were then numbered 1–16 in a certain sequence, so that when fire commenced, the firing would continue alternately along the firing line. The colour guard platoons in the center (H and I) were kept in reserve. In 1748, battalions had only one colour guard platoon. Drummers and *timmerlieden* were placed behind the centre and the grenadier platoons. (Author's Drawing)

were disbanded in the following year. To make the remaining force more efficient and cost-effective, the regiments were reOrganised in 1752; this meant several regiments were either disbanded or amalgamated into other units. As a result, the infantry consisted of eight Guard and Life Guard regiments, 17 national regiments, six Swiss regiments (including the Swiss Guards), three Scots regiments, one Walloon regiment (from 1762), and four German regiments. Almost all regiments consisted of two battalions, making a total of 75 battalions, each of six musketeer companies and one grenadier company. The Swiss regiments consisted of three battalions, each of four large companies (up to 260 men), with no separate grenadier companies. This remained so until 1795.

Battalion and Company Organisation

The colonel-proprietors who owned the regiments left the affairs of recruiting, clothing, and equipping the men to the colonel-commanders and the captains. Each captain received 25 *Rijksdaalders* for every recruit; this he spent on the advance pay, uniform, and equipment of the volunteer. After the War of the Spanish Succession, the State Council abolished the practice of temporary service, making service in the army permanent. Growing unrest among the rank-and file led to the re-introduction of temporary contracts in 1726, since it was easier to find men who would serve a number of years, instead of one willing to spend the rest of his life in the army. There was now also the possibility to leave the regiment after at least six years of

Two prints from a series on the manual of arms, dated somewhere before 1740. Depicted here are two members of a *Schutterij* (town militia). The members of these militias were armed with muskets, bayonets, and swords, although their equipment consisted of a belly box and priming horn. Depicted here are plates 9, 'Give fire', and plate 52, 'Charge your bayonet breast high'. Note the position of the musket when firing, being placed low on the shoulder. (Geheugen van Nederland)

Officer, plate 59 from the series of prints on the manual of arms. The *Schutterij* had no uniforms, although the officers tended to acquire themselves a form of military attire, as is shown here. (Geheugen van Nederland)

service, either by paying a sum or finding a replacement. In wartime, finding suitable recruits became harder, and in 1747 captains resorted to signing up recruits for two years, or even one.

Recruiting was done in the winter months, when there was little or no field work available. Officers had to make sure the recruits were robust and stout men, between the ages of 18 and 32, with a minimum height of 5 *voet* 5 *duimen* (one *Rijnlandse voet* = 0.314 metre; one *voet* = 12 *Rijnlandse duimen*; one *duim* = 2.61 centimetres; about 1.70 metres), the youngest recruits to be at least 5 foot 4 (1.67 metres). The company had to be complete by 1 April. After the recruit had joined the regiment, the sergeants and corporals needed about six weeks to teach the recruit the exercise and the manual of arms. The drill period was from 25 March until the end of May, the final day being stipulated by the garrison commander. On this day, battalion manoeuvres and a parade revue were held. The soldiers usually worked in and around their garrisons in different professions, earning wages to add to their pay; drill days were therefore held on Mondays only, once every four weeks. In September, the whole battalion had to be present for eight days of battalion exercises, also ending in manoeuvres and a parade revue.

A regiment of infantry usually consisted of one battalion of 10 companies; the average strength in the field was about 750 to 800 man, out of a paper strength of 900. Only in the latter years of the War of the Austrian Succession were battalions understrength. The battalions with the most men (700 or more) would be sent to the field army, while the many undermanned regiments, consisting of no more than 300 to 400 men, were doing garrison duties. The Fifth Augmentation of 1747 was meant to boost the numbers of the field army with 30,000 men, mostly consisting of Scots, Swiss, and German regiments. The number of battalions over the years is given below:

Year	1740	1742	1744	1745	1746	1747	1748	1753
National battalions	50	50	50	50	50	50	51	52
Swiss battalions	10	12	12	12	12	12	25	11
Scots battalions	3	3	3	6	6	8	8	6
Walloon battalions						1	2	3
German battalions		2	6	11	17	30	40	3
Total	63	67	71	79	85	101	126	75

In theory, every company should be composed of at least two thirds of experienced soldiers and one third new recruits. After the War of the Spanish Succession, the numbers required for a company dropped, although the number of officers and NCO's remained the same. This not only meant that when war broke out, the number of recruits in comparison to the number of veterans would be too high, but also made the army quite expensive. In an effort to save money, and increase effectiveness, the number of companies was reduced in 1721. Below is an overview of the company strength during the 18th century:

	1713	1718	1727	1729	1736	1740	1741	1742	1747	1752
Officers, NCO's, &c.	11	9	10	11	10	11	12	12	14	7
Corporals and privates	55	35	45	54	45	58	69	78	74	48
Total	66	44	55	65	55	69	71	90	88	55

In 1752, a musketeer company thus consisted on paper of one captain, one lieutenant, one ensign (or *sous-luitenant*), two sergeants, one paymaster (*solliciteur*), one drummer, three corporals and 45 musketeers; grenadier companies consisted of one captain, one captain-commander, one lieutenant, one ensign, two sergeants, one paymaster, two drummers, three corporals and 52 grenadiers.

Every company initially consisted of musketeers (also named fusiliers), pikemen and grenadiers, in a ratio of 3:1:1. Pikes were long regarded as necessary against cavalry attacks, so in 1706, it was stipulated that one in five men were to be armed with this weapon. The pikemen were grouped together in the centre around the colours. Although the pike was officially discontinued in 1709, it was still kept by most regiments during the 1720s and mentioned in manuals up to the 1730s. But Dibbetz wrote in 1740 in his *Military Dictionary*: 'That cross has (thank God) been taken to church, these instruments being transformed into broomsticks and coathangers'; a pike drill was nevertheless included in his book for anyone 'still interested in willing to learn how to handle these useless item'.

Grenadiers first appeared in the infantry companies in 1674; in 1714, it was decided that one in five men was to be a grenadier. The grenadiers were to be grouped together in two combined companies on either flank of the battalion; since every officer was supposed to lead them in turn, it meant they had to acquire an additional grenadier cap, light musket and cartridge box, in addition to their officers' necessities. Grenadiers were recruited among the musketeers, but few were enthusiastic about it. Being a grenadier had some advantages and gave the soldier an elite status, but he did not receive extra pay; instead, he had to wear a cumbersome cap, and had more equipment to keep in order. On 7 June 1749, all regiments (except the Swiss) were ordered to form two grenadier companies within every battalion; from July 30 of that year, every grenadier would receive an additional pay of 2 *stuivers* a week. They would be given first choice when going into quarters, and were exempt of doing manual labour. Also of note is that grenadiers were exempt from running the gauntlet when punished.

The officers of these companies would receive extra pay, funded by reducing every grenadier company by one private. The grenadier companies had to be up to strength at all times; this meant that the grenadier officers could take recruits from the fusilier companies at will, and their colleagues in the fusilier companies could not refuse them, even if that meant that their own companies would be undermanned. This led to much discourse among the officers corps, which proved fatal for overall morale. As of January 1772, the musketeer officers were no longer required to give up recruits to keep the grenadier companies up to strength, the grenadier officers now having to recruit additional men if needed.

Every company usually had two drummers. Already in 1687 it was stipulated that musicians were expensive, and thus, that the colonels 'should not burden the captains with keeping and paying for several hautbois players, fifers and shawm players, other than with unanimous consent of the captains'. Regimental commanders added fifers at their own costs, or replaced a few drummers – or even musketeers – by fifers. In 1750, one fifer was added to the newly formed grenadier companies (funded by reducing the musketeer companies by one man), whilst three drummers of the musketeer companies were replaced by fifers. With 10 companies in a battalion, that means the field music was composed of five fifers and 15 drummers. Some regiments added a number of hautbois players to that, although this was frowned upon by the States General, as being frivolous and too expensive. After 1752, fifers were again abolished, each battalion of six companies now having 12 drummers. The Dutch Guards were exempt from this, having two drummers and a fifer in each company; the Swiss Guards and company of *Cent Suisses* also had fifers, as can be seen on the etchings of the funeral procession of Willem IV in 1753. In the new regulations for the infantry of 1771, each company is mentioned as having two drummers and one fifer; a drum major is mentioned who commands the musicians, including the hautbois players, of the regiment.

Finally, there were the carpenters ('*timmerlieden*'), equipped with a leather apron and gloves, an axe and a special sabre that could be used as a saw. One grenadier in every company could be selected for this task.

Although apparently not officially on the muster rolls of battalions and companies, they are mentioned in several sources; carpenters of the Dutch and Swiss Guards can be seen in the prints of the funeral procession of Willem IV. According to the 1771 regulations, they were grouped behind the centre and the flanks of the battalion, just in front of the musicians. No special mention is made about their dress, other than that they were dressed as the grenadiers.

Colour of the Yellow Regiment of the *Schutterij* of Amsterdam. Amsterdam had four regiments of *Schutterij*, each distinguished by a colour (yellow, blue, green, and red). (Rijksmuseum)

Tactics

In the last quarter of the 17th century, linear tactics and the system of platoon firing was developed to such an extent that it was described by the French as 'la méthode Hollandoise'. During the War of the Spanish Succession, the Dutch infantry excelled in drill and firepower. The drill used for the infantry was that of 1688, albeit that the chapter on matchlock drill was replaced by a manual for the flintlock, which appeared in 1701. Despite the army seeing no action for the decades to come, there were several new exercises and drill manuals developed, which were in use with several regiments. In 1728, the States General had enough of these experiments, and issued regulations, stating these 'new ideas were doing the country the greatest disservice'. Therefore, the 1688 regulations should be adhered to at all times, as well as the 1701 manual. An example of a manual of arms is the manuscript in the National Army Museum by a Captain Bilderbeek, a handwritten and illustrated document dated 1730, that shows the exercise for the Musketeer, Grenadier and Pikeman in the Regiment of Colonel Doys, who took command of the regiment that year. Commanders were again reminded in April 1734 that the manuals be followed strictly, and no changes or improvisations were to be made.

The system of platoon firing required that the battalion be lined up in three ranks, and, despite the number of companies, be divided into 18 platoons, each platoon firing alternately. As one can imagine, this called for extensive training; and when in battle, the first series of platoon firings would be done by the book, until the noise, chaos and smoke caused the platoons, and even the individual men, to load and fire at will. The result, in the end, was a barrage of lead and fire, grinding away the enemy lines, at which the Dutch excelled. The great disadvantage of the linear tactic was its immobility: battalions in line were hard to manoeuvre across a battlefield, which made it virtually impossible to have troops at the ready to exploit a breach in the enemy line. Cronström favoured keeping a reserve behind the second battle line; but it still took a lot of time to bring these to the desired position. The idea of battalions moving and fighting in column was developed by among others the French theorist Jean Charles de Folard, who sought an answer to the superior Dutch firepower. His theory was that infantry in columns would have greater manoeuvrability, and could break through the three ranks of a line with ease. Some Dutch generals, like Lieutenant General Hobbema van Aylva, were advocates for the attack in column formation; in 1740, he even pleaded for the reintroduction of the pike as an offensive weapon. Cronström knew Folard personally: he had taken him prisoner in 1710. He described Folard as being 'a clever, passionate man, with such an imagination, that no one can talk him out of something he has envisioned. [He] is eloquent and persuasive […], but I am convinced that he has not tested one hundredth of any of his writings'. He was convinced that even half a minute of rapid platoon firing at close range could devastate the advancing columns, let alone have them fall back once the officers leading it would have been killed.

Cronström proposed to let the men practice shooting at targets. Despite the ability of the platoons firing with clockwork precision, most shots missed their mark. In 1742, Reverend Meinhard Busscher (1710–1762), a clergyman with an interest in military matters, had successfully demonstrated that the manner of levelling the weapons was responsible for the lack of hits: the manual of arms described that when the men received to order to make ready, they would level their muskets breast high ('aanleggen op de halve man'). In many cases, the bullet would slam into the ground, reaching a distance of no further than 40 to 45 metres. He noticed that huntsmen and farmers usually placed their weapons higher up against the shoulder and looked with one eye over the barrel, carefully taking aim. He argued in several of his publications during and after the war that the soldiers should be taught to take aim as well. The idea was not immediately adopted by the army during the War of the Austrian Succession. The Council of State ordered the colonels to have ten men in each company and the timmerlieden be armed with hunting rifles; they were to be given finer gunpowder, and to practice shooting at targets, with awards for the nine best marksmen. Every battalion thus had 70 sharpshooters. It was however in the new regulations of 1749 (based on the Prussian regulations), that the manual now described that every soldier had to take aim, since 'he must know which way to direct his shot'.

5

The Infantry Regiments During the 18th Century

The infantry regiments, including guards and marines, were divided into national and foreign regiments. During the 18th century, the foreign regiments consisted of Swiss, Scottish, German and Walloon regiments. As was the custom in the 18th century, all regiments were known by the name of the *inhaber* or colonel-proprietor of the regiment. If needed, infantry regiments could be designated as regiments of marines ('*Regimenten Mariniers*'), to serve on board the fleet or in the colonies. These marine regiments would then be garrisoned in and around towns near the coast or sent overseas. Regiments raised as marines could in turn be designated as infantry; usually, marine regiments would upon return to the Republic be taken into the line as infantry regiments. Also during the 18th century, Provincial admiralties would hire independent units of marines to serve aboard ships, but these were usually short lived. In 1752 the city of Amsterdam had raised two companies of marines with a combined strength of 400 men; these would become part of the cities' garrison in 1801. Only in 1763 and 1772 were two regiments specifically raised as regiments of marines, for service overseas to quell slave rebellions in Berbice and Surinam. Free companies ('*Vrij Compagnieën*'), independent companies which acted as irregular troops much like the Prussian *Freicorps*, were raised for the duration of the war.

Since practically no colonel-proprietors commanded their regiments in person, the colonel-commandant commanded the regiment in peacetime and in war, and took care of matters such as recruitment and the purchase of uniforms and equipment. It was only after 1772 that the regiments ceased be named after their colonel-proprietor, but instead designated by their respective numbers (which they had already received in 1752), except for the guard and life guard units. The foreign regiments would be numbered separately.

For those soldiers who were no longer able to do their duties, either by old age or because of injuries sustained in wartime, Holland had raised five companies of invalids ('*Invaliden*'), which would perform garrison duties or work in the army's depositories and stores. In 1752, the 1st Company was stationed in Delft, the 2nd in Woudrichem, the 3rd in Naarden, the 4th

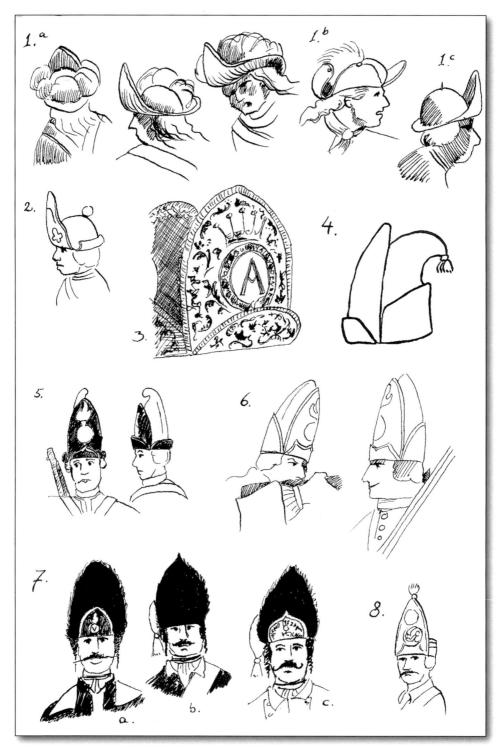

Grenadier cap designs, 1690 to 1754, sketches after contemporary prints and paintings: 1a. & 1b. Dutch Guards at the Battle of the Boyne, after Romeyn de Hooghe, 1690; 1c. Ditto, after Jan Luycken, 1690; 2. Dutch Guards, after Romeyn de Hooghe, 1702; 3. Officer's grenadier cap, Albemarle's Swiss Regiment, 1702; 4. Pallandt's Regiment, 1715; 5. Doys' Regiment, 1730; 6. Glinstra's Regiment, 1742; 7. Fur caps of Walloon (a), Swiss (b) and Scots (c) regiments, 1748–1754; 8. Dutch Guards, 1752. (Author's drawing)

in Clundert and the 5th in Woerden. The 4th Company was relocated to Dordrecht in 1786, whilst that same year the 5th was moved to Loevestein, a fortress near Woudrichem that served as a state prison. In 1795, the companies of *Invaliden* were disbanded.

The Uniforms: Regulations, Economics and Fashion

Contemporary descriptions of uniforms are scarce, therefore, for an idea about the dress of the officers and men in service of the States General, we have to rely on receipts of material deliveries, officer portraits, and, in the case of drawings, paintings, and sketches, often secondary sources. Regarding the latter, there are numerous copies and uniform reconstructions, made in the late 19th century and during the first half of the 20th century, by several military artists, such as J. Hoynck van Papendrecht, F.J.G. ten Raa, C.G. Boode, and F.G. de Wilde.

Since the purchase of uniforms was entirely left to the commanders of the regiment, and regulations from the States General regarding the clothing of the army were mere guidelines on quality, duration, uniformity, rank distinctions, and – above all – finances, the regiments wore a variety of uniforms throughout the century, with elements such as lapels, collars, lace, shoulder knots, and shoulder straps added or removed every few years. Article XVIII of the 1734 resolution stated that a soldier was to receive every two years, in the month of May, a coat, a pair of breeches, a sleeved kersey waistcoat lined with baize, two hats, two pairs of stockings, a pair of gloves, two neck stocks and a shoulder knot. The Dutch Guards were to receive every three years a coat of finer broadcloth lined with baize, a waistcoat lined with linen, two pairs of breeches lined with linen, two hats – one with 'fine' lace, the other 'ordinary' lace – two pairs of stockings, four black neck stocks, and a pair of gloves. The soldier also received 'small goods': three shirts, two pairs of shoes, a pair of shoe buckles, an unbleached linen work smock, and a night cap; later regulations also specify both black and white gaiters and two pairs of white linen knee covers, a powder bag, a large comb, a lice comb, three brushes, and for musketeers a black ribbon for tying up the queue; all grenadiers were expected to have blackened moustaches, the hair swept under the cap, except for two *cadenettes* over the ears.

The States General stressed that the uniforms would be above all cost effective, devoid of unnecessary embellishments and frivolities that would otherwise be a strain on the available funds. However, we know the colonels and captains would try and save as much as possible on the funds for the rank and file, in order to have more money available for embellishments and elaborate musicians' uniforms, often digging into their own pockets to pay for extra musicians or additional decorations.

Regarding the appearance of the infantry, it is safe to say that the cut of the uniforms followed the fashion of the day. The French military fashion was widely copied, with roomy coats and elaborate cuffs, although after the 1760s the tighter Prussian military fashion became all the rage. No particular distinction was made in the uniforms and equipment between infantry and marine regiments, except when overseas units adapted their uniforms to the tropical climate. The uniforms were in a variety of colours and fabrics at the

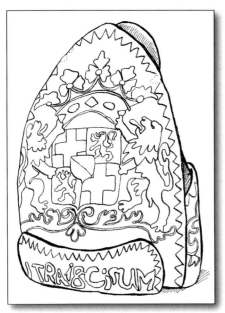

Sketch of the embroidery on the cap of Pallandt's Regiment, 1715, in the collection of the United Services Museum in Edinburgh. The intricate embroidery shows the coat of arms of Utrecht. (Author's drawing)

beginning of the 18th century, although during the War of the Spanish Succession most line regiments were dressed in grey or white coats with coloured lining and cuffs. Blue coats were at first reserved for the Dutch Guards, but were slowly adopted by the line in the first half of the 18th century. The colour of the waistcoat and breeches was sometimes the same as the coat (being made of the same fabric), though more often in the facing colour. Leather breeches had been discontinued in the 1730s, and the practice of wearing coloured smallclothes vanished after the 1740s. Grey and dark blue kersey were the most cost-effective fabrics available, being sturdy and available in large quantities; baize was chosen for the lining, usually in a distinctive and/ or contrasting colour; red was a popular choice, again this being the most economic choice for making cost-effective but relatively attractive uniforms; a print showing the order of battle of the Allied army in Germany in 1743 depicts all Dutch infantry present as blue with red (apart from the Waldeck troops). In May 1752, the regulations confirmed that all regiments (except the Scots) were to be dressed in blue, though it was up to the whim of the colonel-proprietor to have lapels, collars, and lace decoration added to the uniforms, as well as choosing the facing colour. By then, most regiments had chosen white as the colour for the smallclothes, with a few regiments opting for yellow or buff.

The hats of the musketeers could be decorated with false-gold or false-silver lace; after the 1760s this was either white or yellow worsted lace, with gold or silver hat lace as rank distinction for NCO's and corporals. Universal was the black cockade, worn during the Stadholderless Era and now adopted as the field sign of the Dutch Republic. Only when the Prince of Orange became Stadholder in 1747 did an Orange frenzy among the population lead to the wide adoption – albeit it temporarily – of the orange cockade as the new field sign.

Grenadiers wore distinctive caps, the general design of the cap being a stiffened bag with a high front plate, and flaps in the front and back. The front plate and flaps were embroidered with elements such as grenades, floral patterns, decorative edges, or the coat of arms of the Province; after the formation of separate grenadier companies, the initials or the name of the company commander appeared on some caps. Metal badges or plates were sometimes added. The Dutch Guards chose a type with a low crown and large metal front plate. Swiss regiments followed the Swiss design, being a Prussian style cloth cap, with metal badges on the front flap and the little flap respectively. The Scots Regiments received their caps from Britain, thus wearing the distinctive British embroidered caps. After 1750, the grenadiers of the Swiss, Scots and Walloon regiments were wearing bearskin caps. The Guard would finally adopt these in the 1760s. Several national regiments however held on to embroidered caps until the regulations of 1772. The *timmerlieden* in the regiments were dressed as the grenadiers, and were given a leather apron and gloves, as well as an axe and a toothed sword.

The officers were to adhere to the same strict regulations: from 1725, they were to have no lace or embroidery on their coats or the waistcoats (except for the Guard regiments), even if the rank and file did have lace decorations. The distinctive uniforms in reversed colours were no longer worn by the 1730s. The only distinction was a gold or silver aiguillette on the right shoulder, which hung on the back, but not below the elbow; also a gorget, a sword knot of silver lace with orange silk fringe (designated as a 'field sign'), and the orange sash, which could be worn over the shoulder or around the waist, the latter being prescribed in 1768. Gold or silver lace was applied to the hat, though not wider than 2.6 cm., and not scalloped. Grenadier officer caps were elaborately embroidered with gold or silver. Musketeer captains were at first armed with 10-foot pikes, while the lieutenants carried 5- to 7-foot partisans or spontoons; by 1740, all officers carried spontoons, except those of the grenadiers, who were armed with fusils and bayonets. The design of gorgets, sashes, sword knots, aiguillettes and spontoons varied from regiment to regiment and was only regulated after 1772. There was no system of rank distinction, but, as Dibbetz wrote in his military dictionary, everyone with some knowledge of the military could easily identify each officer by his position in the battalion. Sergeants and corporals were usually distinguished by gold or silver lace along the hats, although regiments often developed their own system of rank distinctions by adding gold or silver lace around the cuffs, collars and lapels, or as lace loops. All sergeants carried 7-foot halberds, except those of the grenadiers, which carried muskets and bayonets.

Colours and Musicians

Every battalion carried two colours, made of silk and carried on 10-foot pikes. They were painted with the same design, which was often the coat of arms of the province on one side, and the colonel's coat of arms on the other, although several different designs are known; trophies, scrolls with mottos, and other elements were added. The first battalion of a regiment carried the white colonel's colour and a regimental colour. The foreign regiments followed suit. The Scots regiments changed to colours of British design during the 1770s, being the Union Flag throughout, with a crown over a rose and thistles, with below a scroll reading 'Nemo Me Impune Laccesit'. Two of these colours were taken to Britain after 1783 and are on display in St. Giles' Cathedral, Edinburgh. The size of the colours were regulated in 1752 to be 1 metre by 1 metre, which is approximately the size of the surviving colours in the collection of the Rijksmuseum. For examples of flags from the War of the Austrian Succession, readers are referred to the manuscript *Les Triomphes de Louis Quinze* in the Bibliothèque Nationale de France, which can be found online.

During the first half of the 18th century, the musicians of the regiments wore uniforms either in the livery colours of the colonel-proprietor, or reversed colours. Decorative lace and cords were added. The uniforms were quite expensive, and the States General repeatedly stressed that the colonels and captains would not spend too much of their funds on these 'frivolities'. However, the officers would even dip into their own pockets to have the

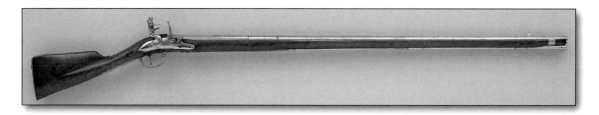

Musket, produced in Solingen, bought by the VOC, dated 1725. (Rijksmuseum)

musicians look as splendid as possible: two paintings of the Stadholder at the Loo Palace, dated 1770, show a grenadier drummer, dressed in yellow and blue. Nevertheless, just like the officers' uniforms, the musicians would in the end be dressed more and more soberly, receiving the same uniforms as the men, and the only decoration being the typical shoulder decorations called 'zwaluwnesten' or 'vogelnesten' (swallows'- or birds' nests) – shoulder pieces of cloth with lace decorations – and livery cords around the edges of the cuffs, collars, lapels, and turnbacks of the coat.

The drums were at first made of wood and painted in the livery colours of the colonel-proprietor, as can be seen in the Bilderbeek Manuscript. Different emblems, like the colonel's coat of arms, scrolls, etc., could be added. The drums were carried on slings that were also in the livery colours and decorated with lace. The later models had brass shells, often with an emblem worked into the shell, as can be seen in some surviving examples. The Dutch and Swiss Guards had brass drums with blue and white striped rims, carried first on decorated slings, but in a painting in 1770 the sling is of white leather, with two loops for the sticks. A drummer of the Cent Suisses is depicted in 1766 with a drum with the rims painted red, white, and blue.

Arms and Equipment

The colonel-commandants and captains would buy weapons and accoutrements for the regiment on the open market. Several gunsmiths and armouries were active in the Republic, mostly in and around Amsterdam, Rotterdam, Utrech,t and Maastricht. Contracts were also made with those in among others Liège and Solingen. During the 17th century, the Republic was the centre of the production of firearms, the muskets being renowned for their quality. One Dutch musket type had the barrel attached to the stock by pins, like the British Long Land Pattern muskets, as can be seen on paintings and in prints. Britain purchased thousands of these muskets from armouries in the Republic during the 1740s; most of these were distributed to Provincial units in the American colonies. Another main type had the barrel attached to the stock with brass double bands. Many regiments however ordered their weapons from Liège, since the mass produced weapons from its armouries were much cheaper.

Despite the muskets having the same calibre, there was a lack in uniformity, not only in design of the weapons, but also in quality. Problems could arise if a gunsmith failed to deliver the weapons and spare parts in time. After the War of the Austrian Succession, plans were made by the newly appointed commander of the artillery Colonel Leonard Stephan, Baron Von Creuznach for a national armoury, with skilled craftsmen using the iron ore from Nassau, that would supply the army with standardized weaponry. To illustrate the lack of quality of the cheap muskets, and the need for a national armoury, he tested 200 muskets from Liège by having them fire with double shot. A third of the barrels exploded after the first volley.

Initial plans for an armoury in Zutphen never came to pass. Finally, after several years of research, an armoury was set up as a private investment by Stadholder Willem V in Culemborg in 1759. The muskets produced by the armouries, marked 'Cuylenburg' or 'Kuilenburg', bearing the coat of arms of Culemborg and the name of the first director Jean Dusseau, were of exceptional quality. A sound testimony to this is the general order for the infantry of 15 September 1809, in which it is stipulated that with the proper care, a musket could be in service for 50 years, and it was not until after the Waterloo campaign that a new musket type was introduced for the Netherlands army.

Orders were steadily coming in, making an investment in material and equipment of 6,000 Guilders necessary by 1766. However, most orders came from the West India Company and several admiralties. Despite the many stands of arms being produced, the armouries were not profitable, as mentioned by the Provincial States of Culemborg in a letter in 1814:

> [H]as the Factory during this 40 year time period [1759–1798, ed.] always performed well and been profitable to the treasury of His Highness? One has to say no to that; […] we believe we must point out the reasons for these disadvantages, the first being the little profit made, since the regimental commanders were not obliged to obtain their arms from this factory, despite their reliability, but preferred to purchase these in Liège and elsewhere for less.

Throughout the 18th century, it was acknowledged that the infantry hanger was outdated. Nevertheless, it was regarded as a vital part of the military apparel, since it was regarded to make every recruit aware of his status as a soldier. His martial appearance could not do without this 'jewel of the military'. Every regiment had a different design, although it was later encouraged that the regiments would copy the sword models of the Guard regiments. Surviving models display several markings, indicating regiment, company and muster number. There was no regulation regarding company colours for sword knots; we only know the company distinctions of the Dutch Guards in 1752: 1st and 2nd Life Guard Companies (Grenadier Companies) – orange; 1st – red and yellow; 2nd – blue and white; 3rd – red and white; 4th – red-white-blue; 5th – white; 6th – yellow; 7th – green and yellow; 8th – blue; 9th – blue-white-yellow; 10th – red; 11th – yellow and white; 12th – green. The strap was of white lace.

The equipment used by the musketeers during the 18th century were a cartridge box, carried on a shoulder belt, and a *porte epée* or waistbelt,

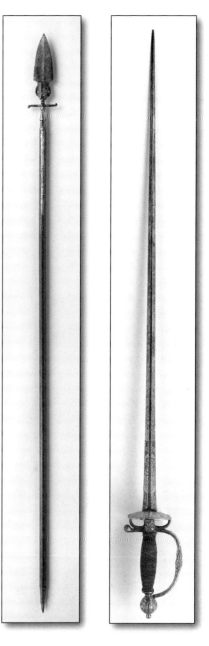

(Left) Spontoon, engraved with the coat of arms of Stadholder Willem IV, 1748–1753. (Rijksmuseum) (Right) Officers' sword with the coat of arms of Willem V, and the motto 'VIVAT P:V:O'; signed by sword master Jacobus Coenraads, dated 1772. (Rijksmuseum)

carrying the bayonet and sword. Grenadiers, who formerly used the large cartridge box for carrying grenades, were also given a small belly box for cartridges, as well as a priming horn and a brass match case. Again, there was no standard model for the shape and size of belts and cartridge boxes, let alone the distribution of them: the Bilderbeek Manuscript for instance, shows musketeers and grenadiers equipped with cartridge boxes as well as belly boxes; Morier shows soldiers of the '*Vrij Compagnieën*' with belly boxes as well, but his Walloon grenadier without. Of his two paintings of Swiss grenadiers, only the one from Planta's regiment is depicted with a priming horn (as well as black gaiters), as opposed to those of Hirzel's, Constant's and Stürler's. Only in 1772 did the regulations specify that the grenadier officers and sergeants were to have belly boxes, stressing the flaps should not be decorated with badges.

The cartridge box sling and waist-belt were of natural coloured leather during the first half of the 18th century. The cartridge box hung low on the hip on a narrow belt, which proved cumbersome on the march, and the loose-hanging cartridge boxes were said to make a lot of noise. After 1752, the belt was made wider and shorter, after the Prussian example. The cartridge box was now carried higher up and closer to the body, and more on the back; the cartridge boxes lined up evenly made a more martial appearance. The leather was now whitened. The priming horn had become obsolete, but the match case as a distinction for the grenadiers was kept. Little is known about the use of badges on the cartridge box flaps, although badges are mentioned in receipts or shown in prints and paintings. The Guard regiments were the first to have a specific belt buckle on the waist-belts, which had a brass rectangular plate; the Dutch Guards had these decorated with the letters 'HG' (*Hollandse Guardes*). The line regiments followed suit, but kept the belt plates plain, without any regimental markings. Following the fashion of the day, the waist-belt was worn under the coat.

The following chapters are an overview of the infantry units, divided into guard units, national regiments and companies, Swiss, Scots, Walloon, and German regiments. Needless to say this overview displays only the regiments active from 1713 until 1772. The name of the regiment is that of the *inhaber* in 1713, unless otherwise specified. Where possible, the names of battles and sieges are added:

1715:	Expeditionary force in England.
1719:	Expeditionary force in Scotland, Battle of Glen Shiel (10 June).
1743:	Campaign in Germany (August–November)
1744:	Siege of Menin (28 May–4 June).
1745:	Siege of Tournai (25 April–19 June), Battle of Fontenoy (11 May), Siege of Oudenaarde (18–21 July), Siege of Dendermonde (8–13 August), Siege of Oostende (7–23 August), Auxiliary force in England.
1746:	Siege of Brussels (7–20 February), Siege of Mons (24 June–11 July), Battle of Rocoux (11 October).
1747:	Defence of Sluis and Sandberg (22 April), Defence of IJzendijke (23 April), Action at Sas van Gent (30 April), Defence of Phillippine (6 May), Siege of Hulst (28 April–12 May), Battle of Lauffeld (2 July), Siege of Bergen-op-Zoom (12 July–16 September).
1748:	Siege of Maastricht (11 April–7 May).

A1

A2

A3

A4

A

C1

C

D

D1

Plate
One

B

Illustration by Mark Allen, see Colour Plate Commentaries for captions and further details.

A₁

A₂

Plate Two

B

Swiss Regts

C

E

D

F

A₃

A₄

2018

Illustration by Mark Allen, see Colour Plate Commentaries for captions and further details.

Plate Three

C3

D

C1

C

C2

B

A

Scots Regiments

Illustration by Mark Allen, see Colour Plate Commentaries for captions and further details.

The Dutch guards exercising at the Koekamp in The Hague, commanded by Colonel Jacob van Kretschmar; painting by T.P.C. Haag, before 1770. Note silver embroidery on the officers' coats and on the saddle housing; the drummer's coat has gold and red livery lace and gold buttons. (Private collection, with kind permission by C. van Kretschmar.)

Plate
Four

A

C

B

D

Walloon and German Regts

Illustration by Mark Allen, see Colour Plate Commentaries for captions and further details.

Plate Five

A

B

C

D

National Infantry
1750 ~ 1770.

2018.

Illustration by Mark Allen, see Colour Plate Commentaries for captions and further details.

Plate Six

A

C

D

B

Infantry Companies 1745–1770

Illustration by Mark Allen, see Colour Plate Commentaries for captions and further details.

6

Guard Regiments, Guard Companies, Life Guard Regiment and 'Oranje' Regiments

The oldest Company of Foot Guards was raised in 1573; the oldest regiment was raised in 1599, being His Highness' Guard Regiment of Foot or Regiment Nassau. The company was incorporated in the Regiment of Foot Guards that was raised by Frederik Hendrik in 1643. During the First Stadholderless Era (1650–1672), this regiment was known as the Regiment of Foot Guards of the States of Holland. When Willem III became Stadholder, the regiment lost its guard status (henceforth taken into the line as Regiment Van Beaumont, incorporated into Leyden's Regiment in 1748). A new regiment, His Highness' Guard Regiment of Foot, was raised, to which the former Company of Foot Guards was transferred.

When in 1674 Major General Van Solms took over command of the Nassau Regiment, he amalgamated both guard regiments into one guard regiment. The amalgamation was probably the result of the involvement of His Highness' Guard Regiment of Foot in the Battle of Seneffe on 11 August 1674. During the battle, which ended in a stalemate but was claimed a victory by both French and Allies, several Dutch units were routed. The colonel-commandant, Count Van Solms and Lieutenant Colonel Cronmann were taken prisoner. Afterwards, Lieutenant Colonel Durklauw was tried and beheaded for cowardice. The regiment thus being without commanders became the 2nd Battalion of the reorganized guard regiment, the Nassau Regiment became the 1st Battalion. This regiment was known throughout the 18th century as the Hollandse Gardes (Dutch Guards).

The Compagnie Gardes Friesland and Compagnie Gardes Groningen were independent guard companies, raised in Friesland and Groningen respectively in the first half of the 17th century. These were commanded by a captain lieutenant. They performed guard duties for the Stadholder at his residencies in these provinces, as well as police duties. A company of *Cent*

Suisses and a body of Court Halberdeers completed the Household Troops of the Stadholder.

During the 17th and 18th centuries, the Princes of Orange became *inhaber* of several regiments. These regiments were named after the House of Orange and the respective provincial establishment. Hence the names 'Oranje-Friesland' (which was designated as the Life Guard Regiment), 'Oranje-Gelderland', 'Oranje Stad en Lande' and 'Oranje-Drenthe'. When Stadholder Willem IV called for the immediate augmentation of the army in 1747 and 1748, four German regiments were raised in Nassau. These were numbered Regimenten Oranje-Nassau Numbers 1–4. In 1752, the Oranje-Nassau regiments were also reorganized, but despite the immense cuts in army spending and decrease of the number of regiments, including the disbanding of many line regiments raised recently with the last augmentations, three out of four *Oranje-Nassau* regiments were kept on the establishment.

In 1749, a regiment of Zwitsersche Gardes (Swiss Guards) was raised, no doubt following the French example. The men were recruited from the five Swiss Regiments of the line. This regiment was in garrison with the Hollandse Gardes in The Hague. From April to June, the regiments alternately exercised on the Plein square, which became a popular tourist attraction.

Although the Guard Regiments and Life Guard regiments were part of the army and were brigaded with the other regiments of the line, they were not numbered (except the Oranje-Nassau regiments), and only known by their respective titles.

The uniform regulations state that the uniforms and accoutrements of the Regiment Hollandse Gardes should be used as examples for the other regiments. The uniforms of the other guard units differed in details, such as the number of lace loops, the design of grenadier caps, and the addition of shoulder knots. The Swiss Guards followed the distinctive example of the Swiss regiments of the line. Musicians' coats were decorated with 'swallows' nests' and livery lace of the Stadholder, being gold with a central red stripe. These changed in size and shape from time to time.

Halberdiers of the Court of the Stadholder

This ceremonial guard consisted of a number of Halberdeers, dressed in ceremonial uniforms, that performed guard duties in the palaces of the Stadholder. Little is known about their origins, although it is very well possible that these were once raised as a personal bodyguard, and later a palace guard to Stadholder Willem III, when he became King of England; they appear in a prints by Romeyn de Hooghe from 1688 and 1691. Prints by La Fargue dated 1766 show a traditional ceremonial uniform, consisting of a long blue *cassaque* that reaches over the knee and closes high up, with wide sleeves closed at the wrist; the whole is decorated with broad red, gold and silver lace; on the breast and the back is embroidered in gold the coat of arms of the Stadholder, surrounded by the order of the garter, a crown above it and below a scroll with the House of Orange-Nassaus' motto 'JE MAINTIENDRAI'. Black hat with narrow brim, with a red-white-blue band around the crown. Red stockings, black shoes with gold buckles, and yellow doeskin gloves complete the uniform.

Regiment Hollandse Gardes, raised 1599 as His Highness' Guard Regiment of Foot or Regiment Nassau. (Holland Establishment).

Inhaber: From 1708–1715, the position was vacant; from 1715 Des Villattes, 1723 Van Friesheim, 1733 Wassenaar, 1737 Van der Duyn, 1756 Van Brunswijk-Wolffenbuttel.

Renamed His Majesty's Guard Regiment of Foot in 1689 until the death of Willem III in 1702, after that known as the Hollandse Gardes (Dutch Guards); the regiment was no longer named for the *inhaber* after 1693.

In 1674 the regiment amalgamated with His Highness' Guard Regiment of Foot, raised in 1672, which became the 2nd Battalion; a newly raised 3rd Battalion was added. The 2nd Battalion split off in 1717, forming the National Regiment Pijll; in 1718 the 3rd Battalion split off to form the National Regiment Thouars (see next chapter under National Regiments AX and AY).

Battles: Germany, Siege of Brussels, Fontenoy, Rocoux, Siege of Bergen op Zoom.

During the time of Willem III, the regiment was nicknamed '*De Blauwe Garde*' (The Blue Guards) after their blue uniforms. The exact hue is not known; presumably it was 'Nassau blue', a colour that was not as dark as that which would be used later in the 18th century. These blue coats were lined with yellowish/orange cloth, with ditto waistcoat, breeches, and stockings. Several prints show the grenadiers wearing a cap with ostrich feathers in 1690.

After 1702: 'Nassau blue' coat lined red, with red cuffs and brass buttons. Waistcoat, breeches and stockings red. Around 1705, the regiment seems to have had white breeches. In the following years, the coats were decorated with white bastion-shaped lace loops on the lapels, cuffs and pockets. The grenadiers were given mitre caps, which later had brass front plates.

1752: dark blue coat lined poppy red, with poppy red Swedish style cuffs and lapels, brass buttons; white bastion-shaped lace loops on the lapels, cuffs and pocket flaps; white lace edging around the cuffs and lapels, white lace shoulder strap. Waistcoat and breeches white. Hats laced white, with black cockade for musketeers. Officers are allowed to have silver lace and embroidery on their coats. Drummers and fifers wear small red 'swallows' nests' with lace decorations on the shoulders, and lace loops on the front. Grenadier caps have a red front and brass plate with the arms of the Stadholder Willem IV, over an armoured hand from a cloud that is holding a sword, below a scroll with the text 'PRO PATRIA'; red band and red hanging bag with white lace; above the front plate a white tassel. Carpenters wear the uniform as the grenadiers, with a brown leather apron and brown leather gloves.

1760: dark blue coat lined red, with red straight cuffs, small dark blue standing cuff, pewter buttons. Straight white lace loops with tassels on the front (six pairs grouped 1 – 2 – 3), and on the cuffs (two pairs), white lace shoulder strap. A painting of a musketeer dated 1762 shows bastion shaped lace loops. In 1768, a red falling collar is added. A painting of the guards at drill at the *Koekamp* in The Hague dated 1768 shows the smallclothes being more akin to ecru than buff, contrasting with the white of the waist-belt and the gaiters. Grenadiers wear fur caps with a red bag, decorated with white lace and tassel; on the front a white metal plate with the coat of arms of the Stadholder. A portrait of Lieutenant Reigersman dated 1763 shows silver floral embroidery around the small standing collar, edges and buttonholes of the coat and an ecru waistcoat. His grenadier cap has a gilded front plate, and silver lace and tassel decoration. The caps of the fifers and drummers do not have a hanging bag, but have another small metal plate on the back of the cap.

1772: a set of watercolour studies of a uniform in the Zeughaus in Berlin shows a dark blue coat lined red, with red straight cuffs, lapels and falling collar, pewter buttons. White pointed lace loops with tassels on the lapels (seven pairs, one on top plus three pairs), below the lapels, cuffs and pocket flaps (each two pairs), plus two pairs on the back. Blue heart decoration on the turnbacks, white lace shoulder strap. White waistcoat and breeches. Hat (model 1771) has a white lace edge, with white lace loop, black cockade, and pewter button; white cord with on each end a tuft of white wool with orange centre. According to regulations, the front plate on the grenadier caps is discontinued.

Compagnie Gardes Friesland, raised 1631. (Friesland establishment).

Also Friesche Garde du Corps or Friesche Staate Gardes.

Uniform before 1765: dark blue coat lined poppy red, with ditto Swedish cuffs, falling collar, and shoulder strap, pewter buttons; the *Jassenboekje* shows white straight lace loops with white tassels on the front (six pairs, grouped 1 – 2 – 3) and on the cuffs (two pairs). Red waistcoat with white straight lace loops, white lace along the front and the pocket flaps, red breeches.

In 1765, the white lace loops are square shaped; hats are edged with white lace, have a white lace loop and pewter button, but apparently no cockade. The drummers have lapels on their coats; the lapels, cuffs, and especially the sleeves are heavily decorated with white lace; on the shoulders red 'swallows' nests' with white lace decoration. The drummers' hats are decorated with white ostrich plumes.

1766: dark blue coat lined poppy red, with red straight cuffs that close vertically with two buttons, red falling collar and red shoulder strap, brass buttons; white scalloped lace loops with tassels on the front (six pairs, grouped two each) and the cuffs (two each), white scalloped lace around the collar, cuffs and on the shoulder strap. White waistcoat and breeches. After 1770, the buttons are pewter again.

Compagnie Gardes Groningen, raised 1640. (Establishment Stad en Lande).

The uniform is much like that of the Compagnie Gardes Friesland, although the waistcoat and breeches are buff, and the straight lace decoration is somewhat different in design. The uniform stays the same throughout the second half of the 18th century, although the *Jassenboekje* gives the number of tasselled lace loops on the front as ten pairs.

Both companies lost their guard status in 1795, and finally disbanded in 1801.

Two prints from a series on the household of Stadhouder Willem V, by Isaac de la Fargue van Nieuwland, dated 1766: front and back view of the Court Halberdeers. (Rijksmuseum)

Two prints from a series on the household of Stadhouder Willem V, by Isaac de la Fargue van Nieuwland: drummer and guardsman of the Cent Suisses, in ceremonial attire. (Rijksmuseum)

Playing card, portraying a *timmerman* of the Dutch Guards, 1750. (Rijksmuseum)

Plate 11 from the series on the funeral procession of Stadholder Willem IV, by Jan Punt, 1753: the Cent Suisses. (Rijksmuseum)

Plate 8 from the series on the funeral procession of Stadholder Willem IV: hautbois players, officers, *timmerlieden* and drummers of the Dutch Guards. (Rijksmuseum)

Plate 9 from the series on the funeral procession of Stadholder Willem IV: grenadiers and musketeers of the Dutch Guards. (Rijksmuseum)

Detail from a print by Rienk Jelgershuis, showing the Compagnie Gardes Friesland at the funeral procession of Princess Maria-Louisa of Hesse-Kassel, 1765. Note specific lace decoration on the coats, and the absence of lace on the officers' coat. (Rijksmuseum)

The marriage of Karel Christiaan van Nassau-Weilburg and Princess Carolina, 1760. Detail of a print by Simon Fokke. Part of a detachment of Dutch Guard grenadiers are seen from the back. Note the style of the hair, the braided hair tucked under the cap and the hanging side curls; the aiguillette and sash of the officer on the right (identified as Lieutenant Johan Pieter Reigersman, b. 1731); the lace and 'swallows' nests' decorations, and the caps of the drummer and fifer. (Rijksmuseum)

Watercolour sketch of a grenadier of the Oranje-Friesland Regiment, after a Delft Blue tile design, dated 1730–1740. (Vinkhuijzen Collection NYPL)

Major Tammo Jacob ten Berge, Regiment Oranje Stad en Lande en Drenthe, 1760. (Groninger Museum, on loan from the 'Protestantse Gemeente Noordlaren Glimmen'; picture by Marten de Leeuw)

Colours of the Orange-Nassau regiments, after 1752. (Rijksmuseum)

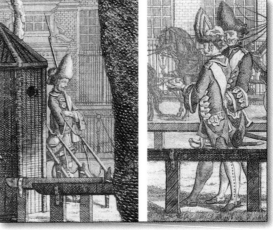

Two details of a print of the Stadholders' residence in The Hague in 1751 by La Fargue, showing Swiss Guard Grenadiers on guard duty. Note the gun rack near the watch house. (Rijksmuseum)

Playing card, portraying a grenadier of the Swiss Guards, 1750. (Rijksmuseum)

Plate 6 from the series on the funeral procession of Stadholder Willem IV: hautbois players, officers, *timmerlieden* and drummers of the Swiss Guards. (Rijksmuseum)

Plate 7 from the series on the funeral procession of Stadholder Willem IV: grenadiers and musketeers of the Swiss Guards. (Rijksmuseum)

Regiment Oranje-Friesland, raised 1639 as Regiment Schwartzenberg. (Friesland establishment).

Inhaber: from 1711 Prince of Orange-Nassau.

Renamed Regiment Nassau-Friesland in 1666 when the Prince of Nassau-Friesland became the inhaber of the regiment, from 1702 known as Regiment Oranje-Friesland, later also as Oranje Nassau Lijfregiment van Zijne Hoogheid (His Highness' Orange-Nassau Life Guards Regiment).

Battles: Fontenoy, Rocoux, Lauffeld, Siege of Bergen op Zoom.

Uniform around 1700 described as blue coat lined red, red cuffs, white laced buttonholes and pewter buttons. Red waistcoat, breeches and stockings. In 1692, the regiment had received 104 grenadier caps.

1731: blue coat lined red, with red cuffs and brass(?) buttons, buttonholes worked with white cord, (white?) shoulder knot. Grenadiers wore cloth caps with on the front a brass grenade and an embroidered decorative edge, on the little flap embroidered 'WKHF' (the initials of Stadholder Willem Karel Hendrik Friso).

A series of officers' portraits dated 1732 show 'Nassau blue' coats lined poppy red, with poppy red full cuffs, falling collar, and lapels. The coat has silver lace on the front, and around the cuffs, collar, lapels and pocket flaps; there are nine silver buttons (in three groups of three) on each lapel, plus two below the lapel; all buttonholes are worked with silver thread; silver aiguillette on the right shoulder. Orange sash worn over the right shoulder. Red waistcoat with silver lace and buttonholes worked with silver thread. One officers' portrait from the same series, but of a later date (1735), shows the abovementioned uniform, but the waistcoat is buff coloured.

1739: 2nd Battalion receives cartridge boxes with cartridge box plates, bearing the coat of arms of the Stadholder.

1740: the regiment receives white shoulder cords with pewter tabs. An officers' portrait dated 1751 shows a dark blue coat lined red with narrow red lapels, each with seven buttons (one at the top, six in pairs). The coat has no lace decoration. The coat has curious falling collar, attached only on the back of the neck; it looks as if it can be folded up, although no visible manner of closing the collar is visible.

1766–1773: as the Regiment Oranje-Gelderland. The *Jassenboekje* shows the coat having a dark blue shoulder strap with white lace around the edge, changed to red with white lace in 1766.

Regiment Oranje-Gelderland (from 1722), raised 1602 as Regiment Van Dorth. (Gelderland establishment).

Inhaber: from 1695 Van Welderen, 1722 the Prince of Orange-Nassau.

When Willem IV became the *inhaber* in 1722,the regiment was renamed Oranje-Gelderland. In 1752, the 2nd batallion was formed by Broekhuysen's Regiment.

Battles: England (1715).

Uniform around 1700: grey coat lined light blue. Light blue waistcoat, grey breeches, light blue stockings, white cravat.

1722: with the Prince of Orange-Nassau as *inhaber* of the regiment, the uniform became similar to that of the other Oranje regiments.

1730: portrait of Lieutenant Colonel Keppel shows blue coat lined red, with red full cuffs and red narrow lapels; silver lace along the edges of the lapels and cuffs, small silver buttons on the lapels in groups of three; orange sash over the right shoulder; hat with narrow silver lace edge and red ostrich plumes

1740: blue coat lined red, with red Swedish style cuffs and lapels, blue shoulder strap and pewter buttons; straight white lace loops on the lapels (seven pairs, evenly spaced), below the lapels (three pairs), on the pocket flaps (three pairs and the cuffs (three pairs); white lace edging around the cuffs, lapels and shoulder strap. Waistcoat and breeches white. In 1751 the regiment receives 69 pairs of silver lace loops for the officers, 417 of the same for the NCOs, and 14,198 pairs white lace loops for privates. In 1753, the white shoulder cords disappear, the lace loops get tassels.

1766–1773: blue coat lined red, with red straight cuffs and lapels, shoulder strap on the right shoulder with white wool fringe, blue small standing collar, pewter buttons; white pointed lace loops with tassels on the lapels (three groups of two each), below the lapels (two pairs), pocket flaps (three pairs) and cuffs (two pairs), white lace edging around the shoulder strap only.

Regiment Oranje-Stad en Lande (from 1718), raised 1647 as Regiment Beyma. (Establishment Stad en Lande).

Inhaber: from 1704, Alberti, 1718 Prince of Orange-Nassau.

Renamed Regiment Oranje Stad en Lande in 1718. After 1752 Regiment Oranje Stad en Lande en Drenthe, when the former Regiment Oranje-Drenthe was incorporated as the 2nd Battalion.

Battles: Fontenoy

Since the Prince of Orange-Nassau became *inhaber* of the regiment in 1718, it is likely the uniform followed the example of the Regiment Hollandse Gardes.

1740–1773: as the Regiment Oranje-Friesland. After 1766, the coat has a shoulder strap with white wool fringe on the right shoulder.

Regiment Oranje-Drenthe (from 1730), raised 1672 as Regiment Van Veerssen. (Establishment Stad en Lande).

Inhaber: from 1710 Ijsbrandts, 1714 van Echten tot Echten, 1730 van Oranje-Nassau. In 1752, the regiment became the 2nd Battalion of the Regiment Oranje-Stad en Lande, which was then renamed Regiment Oranje-Stad en Lande en Drenthe.

Battles: Siege of Bergen op Zoom.

From 1730 until it was incorporated into the Regiment Oranje-Stad en Lande, it wore a uniform similar to that of the other guard regiments.

Oranje-Nassau Regiments

1e Oranje-Nassau Regiment, raised 1747 (Holland establishment).

From 1752 1st Battalion, Regiment Oranje-Nassau 1.

2e Oranje-Nassau Regiment, raised 1747 (Holland establishment).

From 1752 2nd Battalion, Regiment Oranje-Nassau 1.

4e Oranje-Nassau Regiment, raised 1748 (Utrecht establishment).

From 1752 Regiment Oranje-Nassau 3 and in garrison in Germany. From 1767 commanded by the Hereditary Prince ('*Erfprins*') of Orange-Nassau, therefore renamed Regiment Erfprins. Despite being numberd the 4th, this unit was actually senior to the 3rd Regiment.

3e Oranje-Nassau Regiment, raised 1748 (1st battalion Holland establishment, 2nd battalion Friesland establishment). In 1752, the 2nd battalion was formed by the Regiment Baden-Durlach. The regiment was renumbered Regiment Oranje-Nassau 2.

These regiments wore uniforms similar to that of the Oranje regiments.

1753: dark blue coat lined red, with red cuffs, lapels and shoulder strap, pewter buttons. White pointed lace loops with tassels on and below the lapels, on the cuffs and pocket flaps, lace edging on the shoulder strap. White waistcoat and breeches.

1766–1773: The *Jassenboekje* gives the following distinctions:

1st Regiment: straight cuffs; six pairs of lace loops with tassels on the lapels (grouped in pairs).

2nd Regiment: Swedish style cuffs; eight pairs of tasselled lace loops on the lapels, evenly spaced (seven pairs in 1768); after 1770 white lace shoulder strap on the right shoulder, with white wool fringe, six pairs of white lace loops with tassels on the lapels.

3rd Regiment: Swedish style cuffs, six pairs of lace loops with tassels on the lapels (grouped in pairs); no lace on the shoulder strap; the Regiment wore a different kind of lace after 1767, when commanded by the Hereditary Prince of Orange-Nassau, as can be seen in the watercolour by Macalester Loup. Officers uniforms differed in design, as can be seen in portraits from the Staatliche Museen Kassel: a portrait of Colonel Adolph, Prince of Hessen-Philipsthal-Barchfeld dated 1768, shows dark blue coat with poppy red round cuffs and wide, rounded-off lapels, the latter with only five silver rimmed buttons; on the right shoulder is visible a silver epaulette with fringe. In the portrait of Lieutenant Ludwig, Prince of Hessen-Philipstal-Barchfeld dated 1772, the coat has a falling collar, and there are six silver domed buttons on the lapels (grouped 1 – 3 – 2), which have become narrower and squared off; barely visible is the silver aiguillette, and silver floral embroidery on the buttons below the lapels.

Cent Suisses

The first Swiss halberdiers were in the service of Willem III. Their number rose to about 190, organized in a full company. The company was disbanded in 1703 after the death of Willem III, and the men distributed among the Swiss regiments. It is unknown if there had been any more Swiss Guards at the court of the Stadholder in Friesland, but when Willem IV was elected Stadholder of all provinces, a new company of *Cent Suisses* was raised in 1748. The company performed guard duties as the Household troops of the Stadholder. It was dressed in a traditional 'Swiss' costume, consisting of a blue coat with red collar, 'slashed' sleeves with broad red cuffs, and wide blue 'slashed' breeches, both showing the bulky pink (silk?) lining, and heavily set with gold lace; black hat with narrow brim, with red-white-blue cockade and bows, and ditto ostrich feathers; red stockings and shoes with red-white-blue bows; a double white ruff around the neck; yellow doeskin gloves. In some prints, they also wear a cloak.

Officers wore a light orange sash around the waist. Drummers and fifers wore blue 'swallows' nests' shoulder decorations, with gold lace edge and long gold fringe, with in gold the initials 'PVO' (*Prins Van Oranje*, Prince of Orange); the brass fife case and the drum were suspended from a broad red sash with gold lace and gold fringe along the entire length on both edges, with gold carrying cords with gold tassels; the drum sticks were carried in two sets of three gold lace loops that were attached to the front of the sash.

Regiment Zwitserse Gardes, raised 1749. The regiment was recruited from the rank and file of the five Swiss line regiments.

Inhaber: Major General May from raising until the unit was disbanded in 1796.

Uniform in 1750: blue coat lined red, with red Swedish style full cuffs, blue shoulder strap, and pewter buttons; white bastion shaped lace loops on the front, the cuffs and the pocket flaps, the shoulder strap and the cuffs edged with white lace. Blue waistcoat with white bastion shaped loops on the front, plus white lace along the edge and the pocket flaps, blue breeches. Grenadiers wore bearskin caps with a red bag with white lace and tassel. Musicians wore red smallclothes, their uniforms decorated with gold livery lace. Officers were allowed to have silver lace and embroidery on their coats.

1766: the number of white bastion shaped lace loops is reduced to six pairs on the front (grouped in 1 – 2 – 3), and three pairs on the cuffs; edge of white lace around the pocket flaps and the shoulder strap only. On the waistcoat, white lace on the front and around the pocket flaps only.

1768–1773: blue coat lined red, with red straight cuffs and collar, blue shoulder strap, pewter buttons; white bastion shaped lace loops on the front (eight pairs), cuffs (three pairs) and pocket flaps (three pairs); edge of white lace along the collar, cuffs, and shoulder strap. Blue waistcoat and breeches, the waistcoat with an edge of white lace along the front and around the pocket flaps. Officers wear silver hat lace and buttons, the officers' grenadier caps like the men, but with silver lace and tassel.

7

National Regiments

The formation of the army of the Dutch Republic in the second half of the 16th century saw the birth of the first national regiments. Indeed the lineage of some regiments can be traced back to the early years of the Dutch Revolt. Many regiments were raised in wartime, when the need for a large army was imminent, and indeed most regiments were raised in the wars against Britain and France in the 1660s and 1670s. Again during the 18th century, the War of Spanish Succession and the War of Austrian Succession saw the formation of new regiments. However, as rapidly as the army was expanded in wartime, it was as rapidly reduced when hostilities ended. Time and again, numerous regiments were thus disbanded or amalgamated. With so many regiments being raised, disbanded or amalgamated, it is sometimes hard to keep track of the lineage of the regiments. For clarity, the regiments are designated with a letter or letter combination; when regiments were amalgamated, the lineage can be traced through the corresponding letters. Finally, the Free Companies, the Amsterdam Marine Companies and the Corps of Invalids are also added to this chapter.

(A) **Regiment Van Nassau-Dillenburg**, raised 1577 as Regiment De Lalaing van Rennenberg. (Friesland establishment).

Inhaber: from 1711 Van Nassau Dillenburg, 1727 Van Schaumburg-Lippe, 1748 Acronius.

In 1752 it was incorporated as 2nd Battalion Regiment Rumpf (BF), but when Colonel Rumpf died, the regiment became the 1st Battalion, the former 1st Battalion became the 2nd Battalion, and Acronius took over command again. In 1772 designated as Regiment Nationalen 17.

Battles: Fontenoy, Rocoux, Siege of Bergen op Zoom.

In 1738, the regiment receives 136 ells silver hat lace and 114 ells broad silver lace for NCOs, and 48 ells narrow silver lace for corporals

1753: blue coat lined red, with red cuffs and lapels. White waistcoat and breeches.

1766–1775: blue coat lined red, with red cuffs, lapels and shoulder strap, pewter buttons and straight white lace loops (seven on the lapels, three below the lapels and three on the cuffs), white lace around the lapels, cuffs and shoulder strap. White waistcoat and breeches.

(B) Regiment Campe van Bruhese, raised 1586 as Regiment De Zoete van Villers on the Utrecht establishment. (Holland establishment).

Inhaber: from 1705 Campe van Bruhese, 1723 Van Lawick, 1725 Van Boetzelaer tot de Langerak, 1726 Dibbetz, 1746 De la Rivière.

In 1723, Van Lawick's Regiment (L) was incorporated, with Van Lawick taking over command. In 1748, the Regiment Van Outshoorn (Z) was incorporated. In 1752 the regiment became the 2nd Battalion of Kinschot's Regiment (AE).

Before 1700, the regiment wore red coats lined red, with red cuffs, red smallclothes, which changed to 'pearl grey' with red cuffs and lining and with pewter buttons in 1701. The next year, the regiment received white kersey for coats.

(C) Regiment Wichers, raised 1595 as Regiment Nassau Stad en Lande. (Establishment Stad en Lande).

Inhaber: from 1705 Wichers, 1739 Veldtman. Between 1620 and 1625 named Regiment Oranje Stad en Lande, from 1633 named after the *inhaber*.

In 1752 the regiment became the 2nd battalion of the Regiment Lewe van Aduard (Y).

Battles: Rocoux, Siege of Hulst.

(D) Regiment De Chavonnes, raised 1599 as French regiment De Teligny. (Holland establishment).

Inhaber: from 1709 De Chavonnes, 1715 De Carpenter, 1717 Van Els, 1728 Des Villattes, 1759 Holstein-Gottorp.

In 1748, Grotenray's Regiment (AU) was incorporated. In 1752 the 2nd battalion was formed by the Regiment Holstein-Gottorp (AT). In 1772 designated as Regiment Nationalen 5.

Battles: Siege of Tournai, England (1745), Siege of Hulst, Siege of Bergen op Zoom.

Uniform around 1700: grey coat lined blue, blue waistcoat and breeches. Drummers wore uniforms in the livery colours blue and yellow.

1753: blue coat lined red, with red Swedish style cuffs and red lapels, pewter buttons. White waistcoat and breeches. Officers' portrait dated 1754 shows silver domed buttons (seven evenly spaced on each lapel, three below each lapel), and red piping along the pocket flaps; blue waistcoat with heavy embroidery along the front and pockets; orange sash worn over the right shoulder; large silver gorget with engraved the coat of arms of the Stadholder.

1764(?): blue coat lined red, with red Swedish style cuffs and red lapels, small blue standing collar, blue shoulder strap edged red, pewter buttons. White straight lace loops on the lapels (seven pairs, evenly spaced), cuffs, below the lapels (three pairs), collar (one pair) and shoulder strap.

1766–1785: blue coat lined red, with red cuffs and falling collar, blue shoulder strap edged red, brass buttons. White waistcoat and breeches. In 1769, the Swedish style cuffs are replaced by narrow straight cuffs.

(E) Regiment De Saint Amand, raised in 1602 as Regiment Charles. (Holland establishment).

Inhaber: from 1694 De Saint Amand (designated as marines from 1699 – 1711), 1718 Van der Vorst, 1726 De Saint Amand, 1735 Wolterus, 1743 Praetorius, 1762 Onderwater.

In 1752, the 2nd battalion was formed by the Regiment Regiment Lely (AH). In 1772 designated as Regiment Nationalen 8.

Battles: Siege of Bergen op Zoom.

Uniform around 1700: grey coat lined blue, with blue cuffs; blue waistcoat, breeches and stockings.

1717: officer's portrait shows a grey coat lined blue, with blue full cuffs and gold worked buttons; blue waistcoat with gold lace on the front and visible on the edge of the cuffs. Gold gorget with the seal of the States General (rampant lion crowned, holding a sword and a bundle of arrows), orange sash over the right shoulder.

Before 1753: blue coat lined white, with white Swedish style cuffs and falling collar, blue shoulder strap edged white, pewter buttons. Blue hearts on the turnbacks. White waistcoat and breeches.

1753–1773: as above, but colour of lining, cuffs, collar and piping have become red. Grenadiers wear from the late 1760s a bearskin cap with red bag and white lace decoration and white tassel, and a red cloth front flap with white grenade and edge (until 1772); on the cartridge box flap a brass grenade badge. Drummers' uniform, based on two paintings by T.P.C. Haag (dated around 1770): yellow coat with dark blue lining, cuffs and collar, with narrow dark blue 'swallows' nests', everything edged and decorated with livery cord. Yellow waistcoat and breeches. Grenadier drummers wear bearskin caps with red front flaps like the grenadiers, but with a yellow bag and livery cord decoration and tassel. Brass drums with red-white-blue hoops, carried on a white leather sling.

(F) Regiment Van Plettenbergh, raised 1622 as Regiment Von Nassau-Dietz. (Gelderland establishment).

Inhaber: from 1698 Van Plettenbergh van Leenhuysen, 1718 De Bringues, 1723 Van Haersolte, 1737 Van Brakel, 1768 Van Randwijck.

In 1752, the 2nd battalion was formed by Van Randwijck's Regiment (AM). In 1772 designated as Regiment Nationalen 6.

Battles: Germany, Siege of Oudenaarde, England (1745), Siege of Bergen op Zoom.

Uniform around 1700: 'ash grey' coat lined yellow, with yellow full cuffs, pewter buttons. Ash grey waistcoat, breeches and stockings, white cravat.

1743: uniform depicted as blue coat with red.

1753: blue coat lined red, with red Swedish style cuffs and red lapels, pewter buttons. White waistcoat and breeches.

Before 1760(?): as above, but with straight white lace loops on the lapels (seven pairs), cuffs and below the lapels (three pairs). Red shoulder strap with white lace loop, small blue standing collar, pewter buttons.

1760(?)–1766: as above, but without the lace. Waistcoat and breeches now dark blue.

Portrait of Captain Schimmelpenninck van der Oyen, dated 1760, shows a blue coat lined red, with red cuffs and lapels, and silver slightly domed buttons; the lapels reach to the waist and appear to have nine evenly spaced buttons each. Underneath a white waistcoat with silver buttons. Silver gorget with engraved the coat of arms of the Stadholder. Orange sash over the right shoulder.

1767: dark blue coat lined white, with white straight cuffs, falling collar and shoulder strap, pewter buttons, blue hearts on the turnbacks.

(G) Regiment Van Heyden, raised 1632 as Regiment Van Wijnbergen van Horssen tot Oldenaller. (Overijssel establishment).

Inhaber: from 1690 Van Heyden tot Ootmarsum, 1716 van Haersolte, 1728 Verhoeff, 1731 Mulert tot de Leemkuil, 1748 Van den Clooster, 1758 Van Nassau-Weilburg.

In 1748 incorporated the Regiment Van Voorst tot Grimbergen (AG). In 1752, the 2nd battalion was formed by the Regiment Brunswijk-Bevern (BK). In 1772 designated as Regiment Nationalen 20.

Battles: Siege of Bergen op Zoom.

Uniform around 1700: ash grey coat, lining, and cuffs, pewter buttons. Ash grey waistcoat and breeches, red stockings.

1753: blue coat lined red, with red cuffs and lapels. White waistcoat and breeches.

1759: blue coat lined red, with red cuffs, lapels and shoulder strap, pewter buttons and white straight lace loops (one on top plus two groups of three on the lapels, three below the lapels, three on the cuffs, plus one on the shoulder strap). White waistcoat and breeches.

1763–1774: blue coat lined red, with red cuffs and falling collar, brass buttons and white pointed lace loops with tassels (eight on the front in pairs, two on the cuffs); white lace around the shoulder strap and collar. White waistcoat and breeches.

(H) Regiment Van Saksen-Eisenach, raised 1633 as Regiment Van Emminga. (Friesland establishment).

Inhaber: from 1691 Van Saksen-Eisenach, 1742 Van Burmania.

Became 2nd Battalion of the Regiment Van Baden-Durlach (AB) in 1752.

Battles: Germany, Rocoux, Siege of Bergen op Zoom.

In 1743, the uniform is depicted as blue coat with red.

(I) Regiment Van Benthem, raised 1635 as Regiment Van Nassau van Beverweerd.

Inhaber: from 1710 Van Benthem, disbanded 1717.

(K) Regiment Berkhoffer, raised 1643 as Regiment Garde te Voet by Prince Frederik Hendrik of Orange-Nassau on the Friesland establishment, lost its guard status in 1672. (Holland establishment).

Inhaber: from 1704 Berkhoffer, 1726 Crommelin.

Incorporated into the Regiment Van Leyden (AR) in 1748.

In 1732, the uniform is described as blue coat with yellow cuffs.

Plate 1 from Knötels "Uniformenkunde" Part XVI; left: a musketeer and ensign of the Marine Regiment Saint Amand, right: an ensign with the colonels' colour, and a grenadier of Van Friesheim's Regiment. While this print is widely copied, the reconstruction of the grenadier cap (based, according to the comment accompanying the plate, on the caps of the Dutch Guards at the Boyne), is flawed, and any design on the grenadier cap of Van Friesheim's Regiment is unknown. (Vinkhuijzen Collection NYPL)

Portrait of Tieleman Franciscus Xaverius Hoynck van Papendrecht, ensign in Saint Amand's Regiment, dated 1717. The illustration by Knötel was based on this portrait. (Vinkhuijzen Collection NYPL)

Study of a soldier, by Dirk Maas, dated 1700. The appearance of the Dutch soldier would not change much during the first half of the 18th century. (Rijksmuseum)

Detail of a painting by Troost, dated 1742, showing grenadiers in the background, identified as belonging to Glinstra's Regiment. (Rijksmuseum)

Detail from a painting of T.P.C. Haag of a hunting party at the Loo Palace, 1770. The grenadiers are (presumably) of Onderwater's Regiment. The grenadiers have their hair in a braid and tucked under the bearskin cap. Visible is the decorated bag and the front flap, which would disappear after 1772. (Haags Gemeentemuseum, with kind permission of Stichting Edwina van Heek)

(L) Regiment Van Lawick, raised 1655 as Regiment Cuyck van Meteren. (Holland establishment).

Inhaber: from 1712 Van Lawick.

In 1723 incorporated in the Regiment Campe van Bruhese (B).

Uniform in 1701: 'pearl grey' coat lined red, with red cuffs and brass buttons. Red waistcoats.

1702: the rank and file are given red cravats made of 'krip', a silk like fabric. Officers' and sergeants' coats of grey and red broadcloth, decorated with gold lace and gold embroidered buttonholes for rank distinction.

(M) Regiment Baer van Slangenburg, raised 1660 as Henderson's' Regiment of Scots; nationalised in 1665. (Gelderland establishment).

Inhaber: from 1675 Baer van Slangenburg, 1714 Rouillé, 1715 Steenbergen. Disbanded in 1723.

Uniform in 1705: grey coat lined grey, with grey cuffs.

(N) Regiment Van Idsinga, raised 1664 as Regiment Van Hemmema. (Friesland establishment).

Inhaber: 1703 Van Idsinga, 1730 Vegelin van Claerbergen, 1738 Van Glinstra.

In 1752, the regiment became the 2nd Battalion of the Regiment Aylva (AD).

Uniform around 1700: grey coat lined blue, with blue cuffs and pewter buttons. Waistcoat and breeches blue.

1738–1745(?): grey coat lined blue, with blue full cuffs, pewter buttons. Blue waistcoat, grey breeches, blue stockings, white cravat. Grenadiers: grenadier cap with yellow, stiffened bag, blue front plate, blue little flap and blue high hind flap. On the front flap embroidered a grenade with flames and an edge, on the little and back flaps (presumably) floral ornaments and an edge; all embroidery in yellow.

(O) Regiment Verpoorten, raised 1664 as Regiment De Mauregnault. (Zeeland establishment).

Inhaber: from 1708 Verpoorten, 1717 Van Citters, 1718 Van Rechteren van Hemert, 1729 Van Grovestins, 1731 Soute, 1750 Van Swaenenburg, 1758 Van Stolberg, 1764 De Braauw, 1768 Van Raders.

The regiment incorporated the Regiments of Swaenenburg (P), De Braauw (U), and Canisius (AQ) in 1748. In 1752, the 2nd Battalion was formed from the Regiment Van Stolberg (Q). In 1772 designated as Regiment Nationalen 10.

Battles: Siege of Oudenaarde, Sluis, Siege of Hulst.

Uniform in 1750(?)–1770: blue coat lined yellow, with yellow Swedish style cuffs, falling collar and shoulder strap, pewter buttons. White bastion shaped lace loops on the front (six pairs grouped 1 – 2 – 3) and on the cuffs. White waistcoat and breeches. Around 1764–1766, the cuffs become straight; white lace is added around the collar and shoulder strap, as well as blue hearts on the turnbacks.

1771: blue coat lined red, with yellow straight cuffs, falling collar, lapels and shoulder strap, pewter buttons; white straight lace loops on the lapels (seven each, one on top plus six in pairs), below the lapels (two pairs) and the cuffs (two pairs); lace piping round the shoulder strap. Blue heart decorations on the turnbacks.

(P) Regiment De Mauregnault, raised 1664 as Regiment Schotte. (Zeeland establishment).

Designated as marines in 1698 to 1711.

Inhaber: from 1710 De Mauregnault, 1726 Evertsen, 1728 De Blansac, 1742 Van Swaenenburg.

In 1748 incorporated into the Regiment Soute (O).

Battles: Germany, Siege of Oudenaarde, Ijzendijke.

Uniform in 1743 depicted as blue coat with red.

(Q) Regiment Van der Beke, raised 1664 as Regiment Van Vrijbergen. (Zeeland establishment).

Inhaber: from 1701 Van der Beke, 1724 De la Rocque, 1748 Van Flodorff-Wartensleben, 1749 Van Stolberg.

In 1752 became 2nd Battalion of the Regiment Soute (O).

Battles: Siege of Menin, Siege of Dendermonde, England (1745).

(R) Regiment Van Utenhove van Amelisweerd, raised 1665 as Regiment Van Stein-Callenfels. (Holland establishment).

Inhaber: from 1680 Van Utenhove van Amelisweerd, 1715 d'Abadie de Pau, 1725 Smissaert, 1747 Du Vergé .

In 1748, the regiment incorporated Hoolwerfs'Regiment (V). In 1752, the regiment became the 2nd Battalion of the Regiment Evertsen (AW).

(S) Regiment Van Pallandt, raised 1665 as Regiment De Aquila. (Utrecht establishment).

Inhaber: from 1699 Van Pallandt, 1741 Van Dorth, 1747 De Maleprade.

In 1752 incorporated into the Regiment De Guy (AC).

Battles: England (1715), Rocoux.

Uniform in 1703: grey coat with yellow lining and cuffs, pewter buttons and yellow shoulder knots. Yellow waistcoat. For the grenadiers, the regiment receives 130 grenadier caps.

1709: all rank and file receive embroidered caps.

1715: grey coat with yellow lining and cuffs, pewter buttons. Yellow waistcoat. All rank and file wear embroidered caps: the bag and little flap are in black wool, the large front and hind flap are grey. On the front flap the arms of the province Utrecht under a crown, flanked by two rampart lions. The little flap on the front has the motte 'ULTRAIECTINUM'; on the hind flap a crowned cypher 'B.V.P.' in red, yellow and white respectively, plus yellow floral decorations on each side. On the bag a strip of yellow lace on the seam, and a black cloth medallion with a yellow grenade with red flame. All flaps are decorated with an embroidered toothed edge in yellow.

1731: the regiment receives 780 ells livery cord for 26 drummers (30 ells each), and tassels for the drum slings. In 1733, the regiment receives 306 ells broad gold and black lace and 233 ells narrow gold and black lace for nine musicians.

1746: uniform described as red with yellow facings.

1751: portrait of Captain Van Reede ter Aa shows poppy red coat lined black, with black full cuffs and black rounded off lapels, gold buttons (six in pairs on each lapel); button holes worked with gold thread, gold aiguillettes.

(T) Regiment Jacquot, raised 1665 as Marine Regiment Van Ghent. (Holland establishment).Designated as infantry from 1678.

Inhaber: from 1710 Jacquot, 1716 Van Soutelande, 1728 Van Kretschmar, 1730 Meuser, 1736 Heyder, 1741 Tyssot van Patot, 1748 d'Envie.

In 1752, the 2nd battalion was formed from Deutz's Regiment (BA). In 1772 designated Regiment Nationalen 4.

Battles: England (1715), Siege of Tournai, England (1745), Siege of Maastricht.

Uniform in 1766: blue coat lined red, with red cuffs and shoulder strap. Six pairs of white round lace loops (grouped 1 – 2 – 3) on the front, lace edge along the collar, cuffs and shoulder strap. White waistcoat and breeches. Portrait of Lieutenant Colonel Snouckaert van Schauburg dated 1769 shows a dark blue coat lined red, with red full cuffs and falling collar; silver buttons and silver aiguillettes; orange sash around the waist.

In 1771: as before but with a red collar with a white lace edge.

(U) Regiment Van Steenhuysen, raised 1665 as Regiment De Perchoncher-Sedlnitzky, disbanded in 1668 but re-raised in 1672 under the same *inhaber*. (Zeeland establishment).

Inhaber: from 1703 Van Steenhuysen, 1717 Van Vrijbergen, 1721 Balfour, 1723 De la Rocque, 1731 Montet, 1739 De Jonge, 1740 De Braauw.

In 1748 incorporated into Soute's Regiment (O).

Battles: Sas van Gent, Phillippine.

Uniform: in 1740, the regiment received 119 metal front plates, with the coat of arms of Zeeland, and 119 grenade badges 'to be placed on the back' for grenadier caps.

(V) Marine Regiment Van Leefdael, raised 1666 as Infantry Regiment Van Ittersum. Designated as marines in 1698. (Holland establishment).

Inhaber: from 1707 Van Leefdael, 1721 Van Berchem, 1744 Van Rijssel, 1745 Van Hoolwerf and re-designated as infantry, although there are indications that detachments of the regiments continued to serve on board several ships of the admiralty of Holland.

In 1748, the regiment was incorporated by De Vergé's Regiment (R).

Uniform in 1707: a reconstruction by Boode shows a drummer in a blue coat lined yellow, with yellow cuffs and pewter buttons; the sleeves are decorated with yellow lace. Blue waistcoat, breeches and stockings. A red plume on the hat.

1730–1740: all rank and file wear caps with a letter 'M' for '*Mariniers*' (Marines).

(W) Regiment De Villegas, raised 1668 as Regiment Wirtz van Orneholm. (Holland establishment).

Inhaber: from 1708 De Villegas, 1730 De la Gadelliere, 1748 De Villegas.

In 1748, it incorporated Heukelom's Regiment (AA). In 1752 incorporated into the Duke of Brunswijk-Wolfenbüttels' Regiment (AY).

Uniform around 1700: white coat lined blue, with blue cuffs, pewter buttons.

1740–1745(?): uniform described as white with yellow lining and cuffs.

1751: officers' portrait shows dark blue coat lined poppy red, with poppy red Swedish cuffs, lapels, and piping around pocket flaps; domed silver buttons. Dark blue waistcoat and breeches, heavy decorative silver lace on the waistcoat around the edge and the pocket flaps. Silver gorget with the coat of arms of the Stadholder, orange sash over the right shoulder, light yellow leather gloves.

(X) Regiment Ranck, raised 1671 as Regiment Ripperda tot Hengelo. (Utrecht establishment).

Inhaber: from 1701 Ranck, 1712 Rantzouw. Disbanded 1717.

Battles: England (1715).

Uniform around 1700: red coat lined black, with black cuffs, red smallclothes. Black velour mentioned for officers' coats.

(Y) Regiment Van Ripperda, raised 1671 as Regiment Rabenhaupt Sucha. (Establishment Stad en Lande).

Inhaber: from 1703 Van Ripperda, 1722 Lewe, 1728 Sichterman, 1730 Lewe van Aduard.

In 1752, the 2nd Battalion was formed from Veldtman's Regiment (C). Designated in 1772 as Regiment Nationalen 2.

Battles: Phillippine, Siege of Hulst, Siege of Bergen op Zoom.

Uniform in 1703: white coat with white linen lining, white cuffs and brass buttons. Waistcoat, breeches and stockings white. Officers' uniforms were lined red, with red cuffs; sergeants' uniforms were lined carmine red with carmine red cuffs.

1732: uniform described as 'blue with small red cuffs' (presumably narrow Swedish style cuffs).

1753: blue coat lined red, with red straight cuffs with a blue cuff flap, red lapels, brass buttons. White waistcoat and breeches.

1766–1773: blue coat lined white, with straight red cuffs with blue cuff flap, red lapels, blue shoulder strap edged white, small blue collar, brass buttons. The cuff flap closed with four buttons, the lapels each having nine buttons, evenly spaced.

(Z) Regiment Lindeboom, raised 1671 as Regiment Van Smitsburg. (Holland establishment).

Inhaber: from 1692 Lindeboom, 1716 De Savornin, 1740 Van Reede van Outshoorn.

In 1748 incorporated into Rivière's Regiment (B).

Battles: Sluis.

(AA) Regiment d'Yvoy, raised 1671 as Regiment Pain et Vin. (Holland establishment).

Inhaber: from 1704 d'Yvoy, 1720 Van Volkershoven, 1727 Van der Leithen, 1745 Van Heukelom.

In 1748 incorporated into De Villegas' Regiment (W).

Battles: Siege of Hulst.

Uniform in 1701: white coat lined red, with red cuffs. Red waistcoat and breeches. Infantry swords have brass grips. Officers wore white coats with red lining and cuffs, gold buttons, gold embroidered buttonholes. Drummers wore red coats with yellow lining and cuffs, with decorative broad and narrow lace; yellow waistcoat and breeches.

1712: 'pearl grey' coats lined red, with red cuffs. Red waistcoat and breeches. Hats for musketeers with faux gold braid. Drummers wore yellow uniforms with red lining and cuffs, red waistcoat and breeches, hat with faux silver lace. Every man was issued a white linen cravat and red or grey stockings.

(AB) Regiment Van Sixma, raised 1671 as Regiment Stecke. (Friesland establishment).

Inhaber: from 1713 Van Sixma, 1722 Thoe Schwartzenberg en Hohenlansberg, 1747 Van Baden-Durlach.

In 1752, the 2nd battalion was formed from Van Burmania's Regiment (H). Designated in 1772 as Regiment Nationalen 13.

Battles: Scotland.

Uniform after 1700: white coat lined red, white waistcoat. Sergeants wore red coats with white lining and cuffs.

1747–1773: dark blue coat lined red, with red Swedish style cuffs and collar, blue shoulder strap edged red, brass buttons. White scalloped lace with tassels on the front (eight pairs) and the cuffs. White waistcoat and breeches.

(AC) Regiment Van Keppelfox, raised 1672 as Regiment De Baye du Theil. (Utrecht establishment).

Inhaber: from 1706 Van Keppelfox, 1715 De Maleprade, 1733 De Guy.

In 1752 incorporated Maleprade's Regiment (S). In 1772 designated as Regiment Nationalen 11.

Uniform in 1703: grey coat lined red, with red cuffs and brass buttons. A delivery of red, white and yellow cloth, and sets of buttonhole lace, are mentioned, perhaps for the drummers. Officers: grey coat lined red, with red cuffs. Red stockings.

1752–1785: blue coat lined red, with red Swedish style cuffs and lapels, blue shoulder strap edged red, blue small standing collar, brass buttons. On the lapels six buttons in pairs. White waistcoat and breeches. In 1773, the cuffs became straight and closed with four buttons.

(AD) Regiment Van Amama, raised 1672 as Regiment Burmania. (Friesland establishment).

Inhaber: from 1698 Van Amama, 1720 Van Humolda, 1724 Van Aylva, 1772 Van Burmania.

In 1752, the 2nd Battalion was formed from Van Glinstra's Regiment (N). In 1772 designated as Regiment Nationalen 1.

Battles: Germany, Fontenoy.

Uniform in 1743 depicted as blue coat with red.

1753–1773: blue coat lined red, with straight red cuffs and red lapels, blue shoulder strap lined red, small blue standing collar, pewter buttons. The lapels have six buttons grouped 1 – 2 – 3. White waistcoat and breeches. The *Jassenboekje* shows the coat as having a peculiar red falling-collar, which seems to have disappeared around 1766. It also shows buttons appearing on the cuffs in 1769. The lapels are rounded off at the bottom, but become straight in 1773.

(AE) Regiment Van Huffel, raised 1672 as Regiment Jorman. (Holland establishment).

Inhaber: from 1704 Van Huffel, 1733 Van Winsheim, 1733 Van Kinschot the Elder, 1765 Van Cronström, 1768 Van Freyberg, 1769 Van Oyen.

In 1748 it incorporated Van Kinschot's Regiment (AK). In 1752, the 2nd battalion was formed from De la Rivières' Regiment (B). In 1772 designated Regiment Nationalen 7.

Battles: Scotland, Glen Shiel.

Uniform in 1703: white coat lined red, red breeches and stockings. Officers and sergeants a red coat lined red, red stockings.

1719: white coat lined ochre/yellow, with ochre/yellow full cuffs, pewter buttons. White stockings, probably white waistcoat and breeches. Hats with white or false-silver lace.

1753–1766: dark blue coat lined red, with red Swedish style cuffs and lapels (the document in the *Staatsbibliothek* gives the cuffs and lapels as white in 1759), pewter buttons; seven evenly spaced buttons on each lapel. Dark blue waistcoat edged red, dark blue breeches.

1767: dark blue coat lined yellow, with straight yellow and cuffs and falling collar, blue shoulder strap and pewter buttons; straight white lace loops on the front (nine pairs, evenly spaced), the cuffs and on the shoulder strap; blue hearts on the turnbacks. Dark blue waistcoat with straight white laced buttonholes, dark blue breeches.

1769–1774: dark blue coat lined white, with pink cuffs, collar and shoulder strap; white lace around the shoulder strap only, pewter buttons; pink hearts on the turnbacks. White waistcoat and breeches.

(AF) Regiment Van Nassau van Woudenberg, raised 1672 as Regiment Van Stockheim. (Utrecht establishment).

Inhaber: from 1700 Van Nassau van Woudenberg, 1712 De Jonckheere, 1731 Van Rossum, 1734 Van Bronkhorst, 1748 Becker.

In 1752, the regiment became the 2nd battalion of the Regiment Croyé (AN).

Battles: Fontenoy, Siege of Hulst.

Uniform in 1703: grey coat lined grey, grey cuffs. Sergeants grey coats of finer cloth, lined carmine, with red cuffs. Red waistcoat lined carmine. Red stockings, red and white cravats. For rank distinction, red aiguillette with brass tips.

Detail of a painting by Troost from 1741. The grenadiers are identified as belonging to Glinstra's Regiment. Clearly visible is the equipment used, including the small priming horn. (Armemuseum Stockholm)

Portrait of the three sons of Lieutenant General Van Rechteren, dated 1758: on the right the oldest son Joachim Adolf, born 1747, in the uniform of his fathers' regiment; on the left Frederik Lodewijk Christiaan born 1748, in the uniform of an unidentified regiment. Their youngest brother in the middle, Frederik Reinhard Burchard Rudolf (born 1751) is dressed in the uniform of Van Rechteren's Cavalry Regiment. (Stichting Collectie Van Rechteren-Limpurg, with kind permission by N. Count Van Rechteren)

(AG) Regiment Van Rechteren, raised 1672 as Regiment Van Polentz. (Overijssel establishment).

Inhaber: from 1705 Van Rechteren van Westerveld, 1733 Bentinck van Weckeren, 1745 Van Voorst tot Grimbergen.

In 1748 incorporated into Mulert's Regiment (G).

Battles: Siege of Bergen op Zoom.

(AH) Regiment Fagel, raised 1673 as Regiment Van Reede van Amerongen. (Holland establishment).

Inhaber: from 1685 Fagel, 1718 Van Eck van Panthaleon, 1751 Van Lely.

In 1752, the regiment became the 2nd Battalion of the Regiment Praetorius (E).

Uniform around 1700: red coat lined yellow, with yellow cuffs, yellow lace shoulder knots and pewter buttons. Red waistcoat, breeches and stockings, black cravat.

1750: dark blue coat lined red, with red Swedish cuffs and red lapels, pewter buttons (seven evenly spaced on the lapels, three on the cuffs and below the lapels). White waistcoat and breeches. Officers' portrait shows silver domed buttons with silver decorative embroidery, and range sash over the right shoulder.

(AI) Regiment Van Keppel, raised 1673 as Regiment d'Ulsparre on the Utrecht establishment. (Holland establishment).

Inhaber: from 1697 Van Keppel, 1733 Tilly, 1745 De Tertre, 1746 Thierry.

In 1752, the regiment became the 2nd battalion of Lindtman's Regiment (AV).

Battles: Sandberg, Siege of Hulst, Siege of Bergen op Zoom.

Uniform around 1700: red coat lined yellow, with yellow cuffs. Red waistcoat and breeches.

1732: uniform described as white with red lining and cuffs.

1740 – 1750(?): uniform described as blue with yellow lining and cuffs.

(AK) Regiment Buchwitz, raised 1673 as Regiment Van Holstein-Norburg. (Holland establishment).

Inhaber: from 1711 Van Buchwitz, 1727 De Mortaigne, 1731 Van Doys (Colonel), 1742 Van Kinschot the Younger.

In 1748 incorporated in Van Kinschot's Regiment (AE)

Battles: Siege of Hulst, Siege of Bergen op Zoom.

Uniform 1719(?)–1730: the Bilderbeek manuscript shows red coat lined light green, with full light green cuffs and pewter buttons (two rows of buttons, grouped in threes on the front; three each pocket, three on each cuff). Light green waistcoat and stockings, brown leather breeches, white cravat, black hat with false-silver lace around the edge. Grenadiers: grenadier cap with red, stiffened bag, black front plate and black little flap and back flap. On the front flap embroidered a grenade with flames and an edge, on the little and back flaps (presumably) floral ornaments and an edge; all embroidery in white. Officers (and sergeants?) in reversed colours, viz. light green coat with red lining and cuffs, red waistcoat, red stockings. Drummers the same, with decorative livery lace loops around the buttonholes, on the sleeves and the pocket flaps; hat has a red plume; drum is painted in red and light green flames, and is carried on a red strap with lace decoration.

1747: officers wear the sash over the right shoulder, over the coat.

(AL) Regiment Van Brandenburg, raised 1673 as Regiment Van Lehndorf. (Holland establishment).

Inhaber: from 1676 the Elector of Brandenburg, 1731 King of Prussia, 1741 Van Cronström, 1751 Van Holsten.

In 1748 incorporated Van Leiningens' Regiment (AZ). In 1752, the regiment became the 2nd Battalion of Leyden's Regiment (AR).

Battles: Germany, Fontenoy, Siege of Bergen op Zoom.

Uniform around 1700: white with red, with red cravats.

Uniform in 1743 depicted as blue coat with red.

(AM) Regiment Van Deelen, raised 1674 as Regiment Van Wijnbergen. (Gelderland establishment).

Inhaber: from 1704 Van Deelen, 1714 Van Haersolte van Yrst, 1740 Van Randwijck

In 1752, the regiment became the 2nd Battalion of Van Brakels' Regiment (F).

Battles: Germany.

Uniform around 1700: grey coat lined red, with red cuffs. Waistcoat, breeches and stockings grey. A reconstruction by De Wilde shows a drummer wearing a red coat lined white with white cuffs, the drum painted with the coat-of-arms of Gelderland.

Uniform in 1743 depicted as blue coat with red.

(AN) Regiment Van Dedem, raised 1689. (Utrecht establishment).

Inhaber: from 1689 Van Dedem tot den Gelder, 1714 Van Renssen, 1721 Taets van Amerongen, 1733 De Bedarides, 1745 Le Croyé, 1761 Ruysch.

In 1752, the 2nd Battalion was formed from Beckers' Regiment (AF). In 1772 designated Regiment Nationalen 16

Battles: Scotland.

Uniform in 1746: portrait of Captain Paets shows dark blue coat lined red, with red full cuffs and red falling collar; silver domed buttons in pairs on the front and the cuffs; orange sash over the right shoulder.

Uniform in 1753: blue coat lined red, with red Swedish style cuffs and lapels, blue shoulder strap edged red, pewter buttons. The lapels are wide at the top and narrow at the bottom, being rounded off. The *Jassenboekje* shows the coat as having a red falling-collar, which may have been added later. Light yellow/buff waistcoat and breeches.

1760–1766(?): blue coat lined light yellow, with light yellow straight cuffs, falling collar and blue shoulder strap lined light yellow, pewter buttons. Blue waistcoat with yellow piping around the front and the pocket flaps, blue breeches.

1767(?): blue coat lined red, with red straight cuffs and lapels, dark blue small collar, shoulder strap and cuff flaps, pewter buttons; white pointed lace loops on the lapels (seven pairs), below the lapels (three pairs), white lace on the buttonholes of the cuff flaps (closes with three buttons), white lace on the shoulder strap. Blue waistcoat with white pointed lace loops on the front, blue breeches.

1769: Waistcoat and breeches changed to white.

(AO) Regiment Reynhard (from 1693), raised 1689 as Regiment Van Claubergen (Establishment uncertain, possibly Holland).

Disbanded in 1714.

(AP) Regiment Van Els, raised 1690 as Regiment Van Heeckeren. (Gelderland establishment).

Inhaber: from 1695 Van Els, 1730 Van Plotho, 1740 Van Broekhuysen.

In 1752, the regiment became the 2nd Battalion of the Regiment Oranje-Gelderland.

Battles: Fontenoy.

Uniform in 1704: grey coat lined red, with red lining and red full cuffs, red shoulder knot on the right shoulder, brass buttons; red waistcoat, grey breeches and stockings.

1732: uniform described as 'blue with large red cuffs'.

(AQ) Regiment Van Holstein-Beck, raised 1690 as Regiment Van Goes. (Zeeland establishment).

Inhaber: from 1692 Van Holstein-Beck, 1744 Swancke (acting), 1745 Canisius.

In 1748 incorporated into the Regiment Soute (O).

Battles: Siege of Hulst.

(AR) Regiment Van Friesheim, raised 1690. (Holland establishment).

Inhaber: from 1690 Van Friesheim, 1723 De Spaen, 1740 Van Leyden, 1758 Van Holsten, 1770 Hertell.

In 1748 incorporated Crommelin's Regiment (K). In 1752, the 2nd Battalion was formed from Van Holsten's Regiment (AL). In 1772 designated as Regiment Nationalen 15.

Uniform around 1710: grey coat lined blue, with blue cuffs and brass buttons. Blue waistcoat, breeches and stockings.

1740 – 1750(?): uniform described as blue lined yellow, with yellow cuffs.

1753: blue coat lined red, with red Swedish style cuffs and lapels, blue shoulder strap lined red, and brass buttons; the seven buttons on the lapels are evenly spaced. White waistcoat and breeches.

1766: as above uniform, but with pewter buttons; on each lapel one button above plus three pairs. Straight cuffs from 1772 onward.

(AS) Regiment van Cronström (from 1709), raised 1691 as Regiment Oxenstierna. (Zeeland establishment).

De Wilde mentions this regiment as a Swedish regiment, from a contingent of Swedish regiments on the Zeeland establishment during the War of Spanish Succession. Disbanded in 1718.

Battles: England (1715).

Uniform in 1701: blue coat lined red, with blue cuffs and (orange?) shoulder knot; cuffs and pockets edged with orange silk braid, buttonholes edged with orange worsted lace. Red waistcoat and breeches.

(AT) Regiment Van Pruissen, raised 1693 as Regiment Van Brandenburg. (Holland establishment).

Inhaber: from 1698 the Elector of Brandenburg and Crown Prince of Prussia, 1713 King of Prussia, 1740 Van Holstein-Gottorp.

In 1752, the regiment became the 2nd Battalion of Des Villattes' Regiment (D).

Battles: Fontenoy, Siege of Tournai, England (1745), Siege of Bergen op Zoom.

(AU) Regiment De Lislemarais, raised 1701. (Holland establishment).

Inhaber: from 1701 De Lislemarais, 1723 De Bearn d'Abere du Sceaux, 1739 Van Grotenray.

In 1748 incorporated into Des Villattes' Regiment (D).

(AV) Regiment De Vicouse, raised 1701. (Holland establishment).

Inhaber: from 1701 De Vicouse, 1732 De Marvillars, 1737 Vinck, 1743 Van Lindtman, 1772 Van Bylandt.

In 1748 it incorporated Van Raders' Regiment (AX). In 1752, the 2nd Battalion was formed from Thierry's Regiment (AI). In 1772 designated as *Regiment Nationalen 12*.

Battles: Siege of Bergen op Zoom.

Uniform in 1753: blue coat lined red, with red full cuffs and falling collar, blue shoulder strap edged red, and pewter buttons. Buff coloured waistcoat and breeches.

1765–1772: the cuffs become straight and are quite narrow. On the front of the coat on each side eight straight lace loops in pairs, the lace white with a yellow line on one edge.

(AW) Regiment De Montese, raised 1701 as Regiment De Belcastel. (Zeeland establishment).

Inhaber: from 1711 de Montese, 1739 Evertsen.

In 1752, the 2nd Battalion was formed from Du Vergé's Regiment (R). In 1772 designated as Regiment Nationalen 3.

Battles: Germany, Siege of Oudenaarde, Siege of Hulst, Siege of Bergen op Zoom.

Uniform in 1743 depicted as blue coat with red.

1753: blue coat lined red, with red narrow cuffs, red narrow lapels, pewter buttons. White waistcoat and breeches.

1760(?). blue coat lined red, with red Swedish cuffs, dark blue shoulder strap edged red, blue small standing collar, pewter buttons; on the front nine evenly spaced white straight lace loops of narrow lace, three buttons on the cuffs and one on the shoulder strap.

1762–1766(?): blue coat lined red, with red Swedish style cuffs and shoulder strap, blue small standing collar, pewter buttons; white bastion

Details from two paintings by T.P.C. Haag from 1770, showing a drummer of (presumably) Onderwater's Regiment. On the right, the drummer meets his counterpart from the local militia. (Haags Gemeentemuseum, with kind permission of Stichting Edwina van Heek)

Colours of the Baden-Durlach Regiment, 1748–1752. (Rijksmuseum)

(Left) Jan Hendrik van Rijswijk, Major in De Villegas' Regiment in 1751–1752. Portrait by Isaac de la Fargue van Nieuwland, dated 1754. (Rijksmuseum) (Right) Colonels' colour of the Nassau-Weilburg Regiment, after 1752. (Rijksmuseum)

shaped lace loops on the front, grouped in 1 – 2 – 3. Blue waistcoat with white lace loops on the front, blue breeches.

1767: blue coat lined red, with red straight cuffs and falling collar, pewter buttons. White waistcoat and breeches.

(AX) Regiment Pijll, raised 1717. (Holland establishment).

Raised from the 2nd Battalion of the Regiment Hollandse Gardes, hence known as '*Oude Gardes*' ('the Old Guards').

Inhaber: from 1717 Pijll, 1728 Möhr, 1731 Van Doys (Major-General), 1740 van Buddenbroek, 1745 van Raders.

In 1748 incorporated into Van Lindtmans' Regiment (AV).

Battles: Fontenoy.

(AY) Regiment De Thouars, raised 1718. (Holland establishment).

Raised from the 3rd Battalion of the Regiment Hollandse Gardes, hence known as '*Oude Gardes*' ('the Old Guards').

Inhaber: from 1718 De Thouars, 1728 Van Nassau-Siegen, 1734 De Boisroux, 1735 De Terson, 1738 Elias, 1751 Van Brunswijk-Wolfenbuttel, 1756 De Villegas, 1772 Van Aerssen van Sommelsdijk.

In 1748, it incorporated De Villegas' Regiment (W). In 1772 designated Regiment Nationalen 18.

Uniforms: in 1734, the regiment receives 53 ells of gold hat lace for NCOs.

1735: drummers' uniform is a green coat lined yellow, with yellow cuffs, decorated with broad and narrow livery lace; yellow waistcoat and breeches. The regiment receives drums, carrying straps, swords, and belts for 24 drummers.

1753: blue coat lined red, with red Swedish style cuffs and lapels. White waistcoat and breeches.

1759: blue coat lined yellow, with yellow Swedish style cuff and falling collar, blue shoulder strap lined yellow, brass buttons; blue heart decoration on the turnbacks. Yellow waistcoat and breeches.

1767: blue coat lined yellow, with yellow straight cuffs, blue small standing collar, blue shoulder strap, brass buttons; the cuffs close vertically with four buttons (two on the cuff, two above the cuff); yellow straight lace loops on the lapels (seven evenly spaced on each lapel), below the lapel (four pairs), cuffs (on each button) and the collar (one); shoulder strap edged with yellow lace. Blue heart decoration on the turnbacks. Yellow waistcoat and breeches.

1769: as above, but with yellow straight cuffs and yellow falling collar; no lace loops on cuffs or collar, below the lapel only two pairs of lace loops, no decorations on turnbacks.

(AZ) Regiment Van Leiningen, raised 1744. (Holland establishment).

In 1748 incorporated into Van Cronstroms' Regiment (AL)

(BA) Regiment Deutz, raised 1744. (Holland establishment).

In 1752, the regiment became the 2nd Battalion of D'Envie's Regiment (T).

Battles: Siege of Hulst, Siege of Bergen op Zoom.

(BB) Regiment Van Rechteren, raised 1744. (Zeeland establishment).

In 1748, it incorporated Van Ysemburg's Regiment (BD). In 1752, the regiment became the 2nd Battalion of the Regiment Saksen-Hildenburghausen (BG).

Battles: Siege of Bergen op Zoom.

(BC) Regiment Stolberg, raised 1744. (Zeeland establishment).

Disbanded in 1749.

Battles: Siege of Bergen op Zoom.

(BD) Regiment Van Ysemburg, raised 1744. (Zeeland establishment).

In 1748 incorporated into Van Rechterens' Regiment (BB).

(BE) Regiment Van Oyen, raised 1744. (Gelderland establishment).

Disbanded in 1748.

(BF) Regiment Rumpf, raised 1745 (Establishment uncertain, possibly Friesland).

In 1752, Acronius' Regiment (A) was incorporated as 2nd Battalion; however, when Colonel Rumpf died, Major General Acronius took command, making his former regiment the 1st battalion, and the original Rumpf's Regiment the 2nd Battalion. For subsequent history, see under (A).

(BG) Regiment Van Saksen-Hildenburghausen, raised 1747. (Groningen establishment).

Inhaber: from 1747 Van Saksen-Hildburghausen, 1759 Van Rechteren.

In 1752, the 2nd Battalion was formed by Van Rechteren's Regiment (BB). In 1772 designated as Regiment Nationalen 9.

Uniform in 1753: blue coat lined white, with white Swedish style cuffs, lapels, and falling collar, white shoulder strap, brass buttons. White waistcoat and breeches. The lapels disappear around 1755–1758. Portrait of Captain W.C.H. van Randwijck (2nd battalion, 1st company) dated 1759 shows gold aiguillettes and gold embroidery on waistcoat.

1759: blue coat lined red, with red Swedish style cuffs, falling collar and shoulder strap, brass buttons; turnbacks fastened with a button. White waistcoat and breeches.

1768: the cuffs become straight and fairly narrow.

1770: white straight lace loops with tassels are added, six on the front (in 1 – 2 – 3) and two on the cuffs; the cuffs are somewhat broadened, but are cut more narrow again in 1773.

(BH) Regiment Van Imhoff, raised 1747. (Establishment uncertain).

Disbanded in 1751.

(BI) Regiment Baden-Baden, raised 1748. (Zeeland Establishment).

Inhaber: from 1748 Prince of Baden-Baden,1756 Hereditary Prince of Nassau-Usingen.

In 1752, a second battalion (on the Friesland establishment) was organised from companies of the Oranje-Gelderland-, Oranje-Friesland- and Oranje Stad en Lande-regiments. In 1772 desginated as Regiment Nationalen 14.

Uniform in 1753: blue coat lined yellow, with yellow Swedish cuffs, falling collar and shoulder strap, pewter buttons. Yellow waistcoat and breeches.

1759: blue coat lined carmine red, with carmine red straight cuffs, lapels and shoulder strap, blue small standing collar, pewter buttons; the lapels each seven evenly spaced buttons. White waistcoat and breeches.

1766: cuffs close vertically with four buttons (two on the cuffs, two above the cuffs), lapels have six buttons each (three pairs). White '8'-shaped lace loops with tassels on the lapels (three pairs each), below the lapels (two pairs) and on the two buttons above each cuff.

(BK) Regiment Van Brunswijk-Bevern, raised 1748. (Establishment uncertain).

In 1752, the regiment became the 2nd Battalion of Van den Clooster's Regiment (G).

(BL) Regiment Van Baden-Durlach, raised 1748. (Establishment uncertain).

In 1752, the regiment became the 2nd Battalion of Regiment Oranje-Nassau 2.

(BM) Regiment Totleben, raised 1748. (Establishment uncertain).

Disbanded in 1749.

(BN) Marine Regiment De Salve, raised 1763 on the Holland establishment (Zeeland establishment after 1772).

Inhaber: from 1763 De Salve, 1768 Douglas.

Raised for oversees service in Berbice, 1763–1764. In 1772 designated as Regiment Mariniers 19.

Uniform in 1763: blue coat lined blue, with blue straight cuffs and small standing collar, pewter buttons; ten buttons on either side on the front; on the both shoulders a white lace shoulder strap with white wool fringe.

1765: lining and cuffs yellow, blue heart decoration on the turnbacks.

1769–1772: blue coat lined yellow, with yellow straight cuffs and falling collar, pewter buttons; six pairs of white bastion shaped lace loops on the front, grouped 1 – 2 – 3, white lace shoulder strap on he left shoulder only. Blue heart decorations on the turnbacks. Grenadiers wear fur caps with yellow bag, with white lace decoration and tassel.

(BO) Marine Regiment Fourgeoud, raised 1772 (Holland establishment).

Raised for oversees service in Suriname, 1772–1774. Designated as Regiment Mariniers 21.

Uniform in 1772: blue coat lined red, with red straight cuffs and falling collar, blue shoulder strap lined red, pewter buttons; cuffs close vertically with four buttons (two on the cuff, two above the cuff); short coat-tails with vertical pocket flaps lined red; white straight lace loops on the front (ten evenly spaced on each side), cuffs (four pairs) and pocket flaps (three pairs). The *Jassenboekje* shows a buff coloured shortened waistcoat and tight long pantaloons; however, depictions of marines from the book by John Gabriel Stedman show white breeches or white linen pantaloons, and white lace along the collar and the cuffs (although these prints are from a later date and might be an artist's interpretation). In Suriname, the men wore either their hats with the brims down and the lace and cockade removed, or a leather cap.

After 1774, the uniform follows the common pattern and is as described above, but without any white lace, with white waistcoat and breeches.

Vrij Compagniën (Free Companies) (Holland establishment).
Company of Captain Lieutenant […], raised 1745.
Company of Captain Lieutenant Roodt, raised 1745.
Company of Captain De Martines, raised 1746.
Company of Captain Thieni, raised 1746.
Company of Gilliard, raised 1747.
Company of Pouilly de Ginvri, raised 1747.
Company of De Vial, raised 1747.
Company of Bulhlman, raised 1747.

These volunteer units of 75 to 200 men formed the light infantry component in the States' army; they attacked or ambushed enemy columns and provided screens of skirmishers. At Lauffeld, a number of these companies were organised together into a battalion. They had however a reputation for plundering, like their Croat and Pandur counterparts.

A painting by Morier shows three men of three different – though unidentified – companies, each with a distinctive company colour, viz. poppy red, white, and yellow respectively. All wear dark blue coats with lining, round cuffs, and lapels in the company colour, dark blue shoulder strap on the left shoulder, edged and lined in the company colour, domed brass buttons; the seven buttons on the lapels are evenly spaced, underneath the lapels are three buttons. Waistcoats and breeches in the company colour with domed brass buttons. Hat with yellow/false-gold lace and black cockade. Another painting, showing 'An Engagement between French Troops and a Detachment of the Dutch Free Company' gives different views of the uniform, which is green with red. In this painting, there appear to be eight buttons on each lapel; in both paintings, no buttons on the cuffs are visible.

Amsterdam Marine Companies, raised 1752.
Became the garrison of Amsterdam in 1801, from then on known as '*Stadssoldaten*' (city soldiers).
Uniform in 1753: blue coat line red, with red Swedish style cuffs and pewter buttons. White waistcoat and breeches.
1760: portrait of Captain Dirk Trip shows a blue coat lined red, with full red cuffs and lapels and gold domed buttons, white waistcoat. Hat with gold

lace, narrow gold lace loop and gold hat button, black silk cockade. Black neck stock.

1766(?): blue coat line red, with red Swedish style cuffs and falling collar, blue shoulder strap edged red, pewter buttons. White waistcoat and breeches.

Company at Locvestein (Holland establishment).

A separate garrison company that had been on the Holland establishment since the end of the 17th century. Disbanded in 1749.

Companies of *Invaliden*, raised 1725 (Holland establishment).

Disbanded in 1795.

Little is known of the dress of these companies before 1766, but it is fairly safe to assume that the uniforms have always been over dark blue with pewter buttons.

1766–1795: dark blue uniform lined blue, with blue Swedish style cuffs and small standing collar, pewter buttons; six buttons on the front (grouped 1 – 2 – 3), three on each cuff. Blue waistcoat and breeches. Corporals have a single straight silver lace loop on one of the cuff buttons, sergeants have three silver bastion shaped lace loops on the cuff.

8

Swiss Regiments

The Swiss regiments, which made up the bulk of the foreign contingents, were recruited in Switzerland from the Protestant cantons (except the Grisons). The number of regiments differed throughout the 18th century; in 1747 and 1748, there were twelve regiments. After the reorganization of 1752, six regiments, including the guard regiment raised in 1748 and detailed in Chapter 6, remained. The old saying '*Geen geld, geen Zwitsers*' ('No money, no Swiss', from the French: '*Point d'argent, point de Suisse*' or '*Pas d'argent, pas de Suisse*'; in German: '*Kein Kreuzer, keine Schweizer*') to this day means that without money, you cannot buy yourself goods or service.

The '*Regimenten Zwitsers*' (Swiss Regiments) were named after their commanders, although several sources refer to the regiments by the cantons these were recruited from. After 1772, the regiments were designated by their numbers. During the 18th century, the uniforms of the Swiss regiments were also made according to the whim of their respective commanders, but they soon developed some distinctive features that set them apart from the national regiments. The uniform for all regiments consisted of a blue coat lined red, with red cuffs and pewter buttons, in general with blue smallclothes. The rank and file were equipped with infantry swords with iron hilts; waist-belts had iron buckles. Lace decorations were white, although musicians wore yellow or gold lace. In the first half of the 18th century, the grenadiers wore cloth mitre caps. An officer's mitre cap dated 1730 in the collection of the National Military Museum has a blue front plate and bag, sewn together like a pointy hat, with a blue little flap and band, decorated with gold lace around the edges; it has a brass plate on the front plate and smaller plate on the little front flap, a feature perhaps imported from Switzerland (similar mitre caps sporting two cap plates can be seen at the Landesmuseum in Zürich). By the time of the War of Austrian Succession, the grenadiers wore bearskin caps with red bags, with white lace decoration and tassel, as can be seen on two paintings by Morier; throughout the second half of the 18th century, these did not display any front plates. The uniform of the Swiss Guards Regiment, which was raised after the war, followed this example.

The Swiss Regiments were disbanded during 1796 and 1797. In this overview, the regiments are listed under the names of their commanders, with the canton in brackets, Throughout the 18th and early 19th centuries, the regiments from the canton Graubünden are often mentioned separately as *Grisons*, being recruited from Catholic cantons, as opposed to the other regiments recruited from Protestant cantons.

Regiment Zwitsers Tscharner (Regiment Zwitsers van Zürich), raised 1693 as Regiment Lochmann (Holland establishment).

Disbanded in 1714, the men distributed among the other Swiss regiments.

Regiment Zwitsers Schmid de Grüneck (Grisons), raised 1693 as Regiment De Capol. (Holland establishment).

Inhaber: froim 1706 Schmid de Grüneck, 1730 Reydt, 1735 De Salis, 1745 De Planta, 1757 Sprecher de Bernegg, 1763 Schmid.

In 1772 designated as Regiment Zwitsers 4.

Battles: Germany, Fontenoy, Siege of Brussels.

Uniform in 1743 depicted as blue coat with red.

1748: coat has full cuffs, blue shoulder strap edged red, blue small standing collar; on the front two rows of ten buttons. Blue waistcoat with two rows of buttons, blue breeches. Buttons and button holes on coat and waistcoat worked with white cord, plus a pair of white cord loops on the collar.

1753: coat has Swedish style cuffs and a falling collar. The cord decorations are discontinued. White waistcoat and breeches.

1755(?)–1762: coat has narrow Swedish style cuffs, falling collar and shoulder strap, red piping along the front of the coat; blue heart decorations on the turnbacks. Blue waistcoat with red piping along the front and the pocket flaps, blue breeches.

1763: the cuffs become straight; white lace is added on the coat along the collar, shoulder strap and cuffs, on the cuffs two white straight lace loops each; and on the waistcoat along the front and the pocket flaps.

1768: the white lace is discontinued; the waistcoat and breeches become white. In 1772, the cuffs close vertically with three buttons (two on the cuff, one above the cuff), the shoulder strap is now orange. NCOs wear an epaulet of orange and silver on the left shoulder, corporals two white worsted epaulettes with fringe and orange lozenges on the flaps.

Regiment May van Huningen (1e Regiment Zwitsers van Bern), raised 1693 as Regiment de Mulinen (Holland establishment).

Inhaber: from 1707 May van Huningen, 1717 Gumoëns.

Disbanded 1717, part of the regiment incorporated into the Regiment Zwitsers Stürler (Regiment Zwitsers 3).

Regiment Stürler (2e Regiment Zwitsers van Bern), raised 1694 as Regiment Tscharner. (Holland establishment).

Inhaber: from 1702 Stürler, 1722 De Gumoëns d'Opans et de Courcelles, 1737 Stürler.

In 1772 designated Regiment Zwitsers 3.

Battles: England (1715), Scotland, Germany, Fontenoy, Siege of Bergen op Zoom.

Officers' mitre cap of an unidentified Swiss regiment, dated 1730. Formerly in the Military museum in Delft. See also Plate 2. (Authors' collection, courtesy of the National Military Museum)

Uniform in 1743 depicted as blue coat with red. Portrait of Lieutenant Colonel Nicholas Gumoëns dated 1740–1745 shows full cuffs, silver embroidered buttonholes, silver rimmed buttons; red waistcoat with small silver rimmed buttons and silver decorative lace along the front; orange sash around the waist.

1748: coat has full cuffs, red shoulder strap and ditto piping along the front; buttonholes worked with white cord. Blue waistcoat with two rows of buttons, worked with white cord, blue breeches.

1753: coat has Swedish style cuffs, no collar, no white cord decorations.

1766: coat has narrow Swedish style cuffs, falling collar and shoulder strap, red piping along the front of the coat white lace loops on the left side around the buttonholes only; blue heart decorations on the turnbacks. Blue waistcoat with red piping along the front and the pocket flaps, blue breeches. Bag of the grenadier cap is blue. NCOs wear silver lace loops and silver lace around the cuffs, corporals white worsted lace around the cuffs and collar.

Regiment Zwitsers De Chambrier (3e Zwitsers van Bern), raised 1697 as Regiment De Muralt. (Utrecht establishment).

Inhaber: from 1702 De Chambrier, 1728 De Constant-Rebecque, 1756 Stürler, 1764 May.

In 1772 designated as Regiment Zwitsers 5.

Battles: England (1715), Fontenoy, Siege of Bergen op Zoom.

Uniform in 1748: coat has full cuffs, red shoulder strap and red piping along the front, two rows of ten buttons and all buttonholes worked with white cord. Blue waistcoat with two rows of buttons, worked with white cord; blue breeches.

1753: coat has Swedish style cuffs, red small standing(?) collar, no white cord decorations.

1766: coat has straight cuffs and falling collar; white straight lace loops on the front (ten pairs, evenly spaced) and on the cuffs (three pairs), white lace shoulder strap; blue heart decorations on the turnbacks. Blue waistcoat with white straight lace loops and white lace edge along the front and the pocket flaps, blue breeches. NCOs wear three silver lace loops and silver lace around the cuffs, corporals white worsted lace around the cuffs and collar.

Regiment Zwitsers de Mestral, raised 1697 as Regiment De Sacconay-Bursinel. (Establishment uncertain, possibly Holland).

Disbanded in 1714.

Regiment Zwitsers van Milord Albemarle, raised 1701. (Holland establishment).

Inhaber: from 1701 Van Keppel van Albemarle, 1718 Werdmuller, 1726 Hirzel van Wolflingen, 1755 Escher.

In 1772 designated as Regiment Zwitsers 1.

Battles: England (1745), Siege of Bergen op Zoom.

Uniform: portrait of Captain Samuel de Constant Rebecque de Villars Mandras dated 1702 shows a red uniform. In the background is visible a grenadier cap with red stiffened bag, red front plate and red little flap and high hind flap. On the front flap embroidered the letter 'A' surrounded by the order of the Garter, above it a crown, the whole surrounded by floral patterns. The little flap has a grenade and floral patterns. All embroidery in gold.

1726: blue coat lined red, with red full cuffs and falling collar, pewter buttons. White waistcoat, leather breeches, red stockings. Hat edged white, black cockade. Officers parade dress is a blue coat lined red, with red full cuffs and falling collar, with silver lace and/or embroidery along the front, collar, cuffs and pocket flaps, buttonholes worked with silver thread. White waistcoat, chamois breeches, white stockings. Hat edged with silver lace. Service dress is a plain red coat, white waistcoat, chamois breeches, grey stockings.

1748: coat has full cuffs and falling collar, blue shoulder strap edged red. Blue waistcoat and breeches. Buttonholes on the coat and waistcoat worked with white cord.

1753: coat has Swedish style cuffs, no collar, no white cord decorations.

1757: portrait of Lieutenant Johann Caspar Escher vom Luchs shows the coat having a blue small standing-collar, domed silver buttons; blue waistcoat

Colour of an unidentified Swiss regiment, dated after 1752. (Rijksmuseum)

with red piping along the front; orange sash over the right shoulder; small silver engraved gorget (for a lieutenant).

1766: coat has Swedish style cuffs and shoulder strap, blue small standing collar, red piping along the front of the coat; blue heart decorations on the turnbacks. Blue waistcoat with red piping, blue breeches.

1769: the red piping disappears; white pointed lace loops on the front (six pairs, grouped in pairs) and the cuffs, white lace shoulder strap; on the waistcoat white pointed lace loops plus white lace along the front and the cuff flaps. In 1772, a red falling collar is added. NCOs wore silver lace around the cuffs, corporals wore two white worsted epaulettes with fringe.

Regiment Zwitsers De Diesbach, raised 1711. (Holland establishment).
Disbanded in 1714.

Regiment Zwitsers Stürler (Regiment Zwitsers der Kleine Kantons), raised 1748. (Holland establishment.)
Inhaber: from 1748 Stürler, 1756 Bouquet.
In 1749, the Regiment Zwitsers Chambrier was incorporated. In 1772 designated as Regiment Zwitsers 2.
Uniform in 1753: coat has Swedish style cuffs. Blue waistcoat and breeches.
1766: coat has red straight cuffs, blue shoulder strap and blue small standing collar; white pointed lace loops on the front (11 pairs, evenly spaced) and cuffs, white lace edge along the shoulder strap. Blue waistcoat with white pointed lace loops on the front and white lace along the pocket flaps, blue breeches.
1768–1773: a red falling collar is added; the number of lace loops on the front is reduced to nine pairs; the white lace edge along the pocket flaps of the waistcoat is discontinued. NCOs wore silver lace loops (nine pairs on the front, three on the cuffs, three on the pockets and three in the back, plus silver hat lace. Corporals wore two white worsted epaulettes with fringe.

Regiment Zwitsers Budé, raised 1748.
Disbanded in 1749.

Regiment Zwitsers De Graffenriedt, raised 1748. (Establishment uncertain, possibly Holland).
Disbanded in 1749.

Regiment Zwitsers De Chambrier, raised 1748. (Establishment uncertain, possibly Holland).
In 1749 incorporated into the Regiment Zwitsers Stürler (Regiment Zwitsers 2).

Compagnie Zwitserse Jagers, raised 1748.
Attached to De Chambrier's regiment was a Light Company, commanded by Captain Lulin. It was disbanded in 1749.

9

Scottish Regiments

Scottish regiments had been part of the army of the Republic from its very beginning. A large number of regiments had been taken into service during the War of Spanish Succession. After the war, the three oldest regiments were kept in service and formed the *'Schotse Brigade'* (Scots Brigade). These regiments were in fact hired from Britain: the officers swore allegiance to the King of Great Britain, and wore crimson sashes and British gorgets, as can be seen in an officer's portrait dated 1767. The colours carried by the regiments followed the Dutch design, although by the 1770s they carried British colours (examples of these are still on display in St. Giles cathedral in Edinburgh). In 1747, a fourth regiment (Drumlanrig's) was about to be taken into service, but never completed; it was reduced to one battalion in 1749, and disbanded in 1752, the remaining companies added to Halkett's Regiment.

Britain could recall the regiments if it wanted to, as was stipulated in the agreement with the Republic. The Scots Brigade was not recalled during the Jacobite Rebellions in 1715 and 1745, but there were intentions to do so during the Seven Years War, and when the American War of Independence broke out. By then, the relationship between the two nations had deteriorated as such, that within the States General, the opposition – firmly taking the side of the Continentals – refused to allow the Scots Brigade to be sent back to Britain.

The most distinctive feature of the uniforms of the Scottish regiments had been the red coat, which was confirmed in the regulations of 1752. In the first decades of the 18th century, all cloth, buttons, grenadier caps and lace decoration were delivered by Britain. After 1752 , the uniforms were more patterned like the national regiments; the grenadiers wore bearskin caps from 1750 onward, like the other foreign regiments. The regiments had recruited actively in Scotland, as was stipulated in the conventions signed at the end of the 17th century, until this was no longer permitted in 1756; after that, more and more Dutch and German recruits filled the ranks, and even the officer corps was no longer exclusively Scottish. In 1783, during the Fourth English War, the regiments were nationalised, becoming National Regiments 22, 23, and 24.

Regiment Schotten Murray, raised 1595 as Regiment Murray. (Holland establishment).

Inhaber: from 1697 Murray of Melgum, 1719 Cunningham, 1733 Lamy of Dunkenny, 1742 Mackay, 1745 Marjoribanks.

In 1772 designated as Regiment Schotten 1. In 1783 nationalised as Regiment Nationalen 22.

Battles: Siege of Tournai, Rocoux, Lauffeld, Siege of Bergen op Zoom.

Uniform in 1712: white coat lined red, with red cuffs.

1740: red coat lined white, with white cuffs and falling collar, and pewter buttons. White waistcoat and breeches. Hat with false-silver braid.

1745–1749: as above, but with yellow lining, full cuffs, collar and smallclothes.

1753: red coat lined white, with white Swedish style cuffs and lapels, red shoulder strap edged white, pewter buttons. White waistcoat and breeches. Grenadiers: three stripes of white lace with red worm and tassels on each upper arm, and two ditto below the lapels; bearskin cap with red front flap, on it a thistle and the motto 'Nemo : Me : Impune : Lacessit' in white, red bag with white lace decoration and tassel. In 1755, the regiment received 726 ells of 'wide lace' for grenadiers and drummers.

1759: red coat lined white, with white straight cuffs and falling collar, red shoulder strap edged white, pewter buttons; six pairs of white bastion shaped lace loops on the front, red heart decoration on the turnbacks. Grenadiers: three stripes of white lace with red worm and tassels on each upper arm. Officer portrait by Kaldenbach dated 1767 shows scarlet coat lined white, with white straight cuffs and falling collar, silver flat buttons; buttonholes on the front are worked with red silk; the cuffs close vertically with two buttons. White waistcoat with small silver buttons, white breeches. Silver British gorget, carmine sash worn around the waist. Black cravat.

1771: as above, but the laced loops on the front of the coat now have tassels; the distinctive white lace with red worm is no longer in use.

Regiment Schotten Lauder, raised 1603 as Regiment Scott of Bucleuch. (Holland establishment).

From 1689 Lauder, 1716 Halkett, 1742 De Villegas, 1746 Stuart.

In 1772 designated as Regiment Schotten 3. In 1783 nationalised as Regiment Nationalen 24.

Battles: Siege of Dendermonde, Rocoux.

Uniform in 1732–1739: red coat lined yellow, with yellow cuffs; yellow waistcoat and breeches. In 1739, the regiment receives 160 dozen lace loops for the grenadiers.

1746: red coat lined yellow, with yellow cuffs and falling collar; yellow waistcoat and breeches. Musketeers wear 'English model' embroidered fusilier caps instead of hats.

1753: red coat lined yellow, with yellow Swedish style cuffs and lapels, red shoulder strap edged yellow, and pewter buttons. Yellow waistcoat and breeches. Grenadiers: three stripes of yellow lace with red worm and tassels on each upper arm, and two more below the lapels.

Colonel's colour of a Scots regiment, presumably Marjoribanks, second half 18th Century. (Rijksmuseum)

Detail of an unfinished mural at the Fortress Loevestein, showing the bearskin cap of a grenadier of Marjoribanks' Regiment which was stationed there from 1752 to 1754. Note also the side curls and blackened moustache. (Authors' collection)

1759–1772: red coat lined yellow, with yellow straight cuffs and lapels, red shoulder strap edged yellow, and pewter buttons. The cuffs close with a vertical cuff flap with three buttons; after 1766[?] the cuff flaps have yellow piping and close with four buttons. Lapels, cuff flaps and shoulder strap have white straight lace loops. The lapel has seven buttons, one near the collar and six in three pairs. Also later added are red hearts on the turnbacks. Yellow waistcoat and breeches. Grenadiers: three stripes of yellow lace with red worm and tassels on each upper arm, and two more below the lapels.

Regiment Schotten Colyear, raised 1675 as Regiment Colyear. (Holland Establishement).

Inhaber: from 1695 Colyear, 1748 Halkett, 1758 Gordon.

In 1752, the 2nd Battalion was formed by incorporation of the Regiment Drumlanrig. In 1772 designated as Regiment Schotten 2, in 1783 nationalised as Regiment Nationalen 23.

Battles: Rocoux, Lauffeld, Siege of Hulst, Siege of Bergen op Zoom.

Uniform around 1700: red coat with white lining and cuffs.

1731: red coat lined yellow, yellow cuffs and pewter buttons. Grey stockings. Officers and sergeants wear poppy red coats lined yellow, with yellow cuffs; the officers have gold buttons. Drummers wear green coats lined orange, with orange cuffs.

1735: red coat lined yellow, yellow cuffs and brass buttons. Hats have false-gold braid. 108 embroidered grenadier caps are delivered to the regiment.

1746: officers' sashes are orange instead of crimson.

1753: red coat lined yellow, yellow Swedish style cuffs and lapels, red shoulder strap edged yellow, and brass buttons. Yellow waistcoat and breeches. Grenadiers: three stripes of yellow lace with red worm and tassels on each upper arm, and two more below the lapels.

1757–1772: red coat lined white, with dark green Swedish style cuffs and lapels, pewter buttons. White waistcoat and breeches. Grenadiers: three stripes of white lace with green worm and tassels on each upper arm, and two more below the lapels, shoulder straps are decorated with a strip of ditto lace and white wool fringe.

Regiment Schotten Wood, raised 1697 as Regiment Strathnaver of Sutherland. (Utrecht establishment).

Discharged from service in 1717.

Regiment Schotten Hamilton, raised 1697. (Holland establishment).

Discharged from service in 1698. Taken into service again in 1701, discharged in 1714.

Regiment Schotten Douglas (from 1709), raised 1701 as Regiment Colyear of Portmore. (Holland establishment).

Discharged from service in 1717.

Uniform in 1705: red coats with yellow lining and cuffs. Embroidered 'fusilier caps' (sent from Britain), displaying two rampant lions at a rock in natural colours, and the motto 'FIRM'. For grenadiers embroidered grenadier caps, the design like those of the fusiliers, but with a grenade and a 'gun' (a cannon?) in red and blue added.

1706: the fusilier caps are first replaced by hats, but then new fusilier caps are distributed. These have embroidered on them a lion holding arrows, a hand with a sword, a horse, grenades and cannon and the motto 'GRATUS ESTO'. For grenadiers the same, but with the initials of the commander J.H. (for John Hepburn) added.

1711: fusilier caps and drums described as having the emblem of the commander (Douglas), being a bleeding heart and a crown.

Regiment Schotten Drumlanrig, raised 1747. (Holland establishment).

Disbanded in 1752; remaining companies became 2nd Battalion of Halkett's Regiment (see Regiment Schotten Colyear).

Uniform was a red coat lined yellow, with yellow Swedish style cuffs and lapels, red shoulder strap edged yellow. Yellow waistcoat and breeches.

10

Walloon and German Regiments

The Walloon Regiments

During the 17th and 18th centuries, there was one Walloon regiment in service of the Dutch Republic. Its origins lay in the Dutch revolt: in 1600, the regiment was in service of Spain and part of the garrison of Fort Sint Andries in Heerewaarden, built as part of the Spanish siege of Zaltbommel. The Walloon regiment and other units of the garrison started to revolt because they had not received any wages in about three years. The men chased the officers and their families away, and plundered the governor's mansion. The fortress eventually surrendered to Prince Maurice of Orange Nassau. In exchange, the Walloon regiment demanded a payment and to be taken up in the army of the States General, with the Prince of Nassau to become their inhaber, to which Prince Maurice agreed. Having no orange sashes available for the officers and sergeants on such short notice, the officers of the Walloon regiment wore their red sashes over the left shoulder instead of over the right shoulder, not only to show they changed sides, but also to mock the Spanish. Two months later, the regiment distinguished itself in the battle of Nieuwpoort against the Spanish army.

The regiment was put on the Holland establishment and remained in service of the States General throughout the 17th and 18th century. Recruits came from the Austrian Netherlands and the Bishopric of Liege. As stipulated in 1600, the inhaber was always to be from Wallonia. The red sash for officers remained a regimental tradition at least during the 17th century, as the regiment received 48 red sashes for officers in 1690. The dire situation in 1747 called for additional regiments to be taken into service, but after a decade, the remaining regiments, all on the Holland establishment, consisted of no more than one battalion each, and were finally amalgamated with the oldest regiment of Lillers into one regiment of three battalions in 1762. Since these regiments were all commanded by the same inhaber, it is likely they all wore the same uniform.

Regarding the uniform of the Walloon Regiment, there are some references that describe it as grey early in the 18th century. By the time of the

War of Austrian Succession, the regiment wore blue uniforms with white, as can be seen on a painting by Morier dated 1748. This would remain the colour of choice throughout the 18th century. When a battalion of Walloon Guards was raised in 1793 (Bataljon Gardewalen), the uniform chosen for the unit was also blue with white.

Regiment Walen De Hertaing, raised 1600 by Frederik Hendrik count of Nassau.

Inhaber: from 1710 De Hertaing van Marquette, 1723 De Caris, 1737 Van Friesheim, 1742 Smissaert, 1752 Van Lillers, 1762 Smissaert.

In 1762, the 2nd and 3rd battalions were formed by incorporating both Walloon regiments that Lillers commanded.

Battles: Fontenoy, Siege of Brussels, Siege of Bergen op Zoom.

Uniform in 1701: white coat lined red with red cuffs, pewter buttons. White waistcoat and breeches, red stockings. Drummers and grenadiers probably had lace decorations, since the regiment received 384 dozen lace loops. Officers wore carmine red lining and cuffs.

Until 1740: references are made about the regiment being dressed in grey.

1748: blue coat lined white, with white cuffs, small standing collar and brass buttons, marked 'V'. White waistcoat with two rows of buttons, blue breeches. A painting by Morier of a grenadier shows the coat as having a large white falling collar, which can be turned up and closed in front with three buttons. He wears a bearskin cap with a blue front flap with a faux silver edge and a (white?) metal grenade badge, marked 'V', and a blue bag with false-silver lace decoration and tassel. A receipt from 1751 confirms this.

1753: blue coat lined white, with white cuffs and pewter buttons. White waistcoat and breeches.

1755(?)–1760: blue coat lined red, with red cuffs and lapels, blue edged red shoulder strap, brass buttons, white waistcoat and breeches.

1761(?): blue coat lined white, with white round cuffs (closing with two buttons), blue shoulder strap edged white, pewter buttons. White waistcoat and breeches.

1763: blue coat lined blue, with blue standing collar, red Swedish cuffs, white bastion shaped lace loops (ten pairs on the front, one on the collar, two on the cuffs), pewter buttons. White waistcoat and breeches.

1767: blue coat lined white, with white round cuffs, blue standing collar, white pointed lace loops (10 pairs on the front, one on the collar), pewter buttons. Blue waistcoat with white lace around the front and the pocket flaps; blue breeches.

1769–1773: lace decoration is discontinued, except for the shoulder strap; white waistcoat and breeches.

Regiment Walen Cornabé, raised 1747 as Regiment Waalse Dragonders Cornabé.

Inhaber: from 1747 Cornabé, 1752 Lillers.

Raised in April 1747 as a regiment of dragoons, but designated as infantry two months later.

In 1762, the regiment became the 2nd Battalion of the Regiment Walen Smissaert.

Battles: Lauffeld.

Regiment Walen Lillers, raised 1747.

In 1762, the regiment became the 3rd Battalion of the Regiment Walen Smissaert.

Regiment Grenadiers Du Cailla, raised 1749.

Raised as a French regiment, but later known as Waalse Grenadiers.

During the War of the Austrian Succession, Protestant French officers, mostly reformed converts, had fled to the Republic. They had offered to raise a regiment of grenadiers, with a strength of 10 companies; the regiment was to be recruited from French protestant deserters. It was eventually raised after the war and commanded by Colonel Pepin du Cailla. The regiment was reduced in 1751 and finally disbanded in 1752.

German Regiments

The States General usually entered into subsidy treaties with the smaller German states, like Britain did with the Hessian princes during the 18th century. Nevertheless, a number of German battalions from Nassau, Waldeck, and Saxe-Gotha were raised during the War of Austrian Succession and kept in service afterwards. The Nassau Regiments, known as Regimenten Oranje-Nassau, have been discussed earlier along with the guard units.

In 1795, the Batavian Republic, following the French example, wanted to disband all foreign regiments which they regarded as part of the Ancien Régime. Although the Swiss regiments were disbanded fairly early during 1795 and 1796, the government kept the German regiments because the German princes would not be able to pay their wages anymore. General Daendels wrote in a letter that 'National Justice' did not allow them to send the German soldiers back into a life of poverty, since they had 'shed their blood for the Republic [of the United Netherlands], have never taken part in political affairs, and have always served with loyalty and honesty'

The Waldeck regiments wore either white or blue uniforms, but were dressed similar after 1770 in blue with yellow; when a 5th Battalion of Waldeck infantry was raised in 1784, for service in Germany, it wore a similar uniform. The regiment of Saxe-Gotha wore blue with red throughout the 18th century. The German regiments would wear these uniforms until they were incorporated into the Dutch line regiments of the Kingdom of Holland in 1806.

1e Bataljon van Waldeck, raised 1742. (Holland establishment).

Inhaber: from 1742 Karl August Fürst von Waldeck, 1763 Friedrich Fürst von Waldeck.

In 1762 became the 1e Regiment van Waldeck; the 2nd Waldeck Battalion was added as its second battalion. In 1806 incorporated as the 3rd Battalion, 1st Infantry Regiment of the Batavian Republic.

Battles: Germany, Fontenoy, Rocoux, Lauffeld.

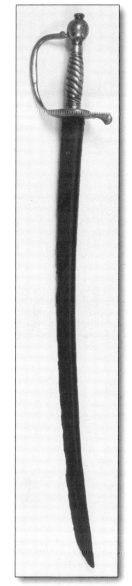

Sabre of the 2nd Waldeck Regiment, marked '2TE REGE WALDECK B No 48' (2e Regiment Waldeck, company B, nr. 48), after 1763. (Rijksmuseum)

Uniform depicted in 1743 as white coat with red.

1753: blue coat lined red, with red Swedish style cuffs and falling collar, brass buttons. Yellow waistcoat and breeches. The Jassenboekje shows a red shoulder strap on the coat, and white waistcoat and breeches.

1768: blue coat lined yellow, with yellow straight cuffs, lapels, falling collar and shoulder strap, and brass buttons; the lapels have seven evenly spaced buttons each. White waistcoat and breeches.

1771: coat as above, but with pewter buttons; cuffs close vertically with two buttons; on the lapel six buttons grouped 1 – 2 – 3.

2e Bataljon van Waldeck, raised 1742. (Holland establishment).
Inhaber: from 1742 Karl August Fürst von Waldeck.
In 1762, the battalion became the second battalion of the 1e Regiment van Waldeck.
Battles: Fontenoy, Rocoux, Lauffeld.
Uniform probably the same as 1st Waldeck Battalion until it was incorporated into the 1st Regiment in 1762.

3e Bataljon van Waldeck, raised 1744. (Holland establishment).
Inhaber: from 1744 Karl August Fürst von Waldeck, 1763 Friedrich Fürst von Waldeck.
In 1763 organised into a regiment, renumbered 2e Regiment van Waldeck.
Battles: Siege of Bergen op Zoom.
Uniform in 1753: white coat lined white, with red Swedish style cuffs and falling collar, brass buttons. White waistcoat and breeches. The Jassenboekje shows red lining, straight cuffs and a red shoulder strap.

1768: white coat lined red, with red narrow straight cuffs, lapels and shoulder strap, brass buttons; the lapels have seven evenly spaced buttons each. White waistcoat and breeches.

1770: blue coat lined yellow, with yellow straight cuffs, lapels, falling collar, and shoulder strap; pewter buttons; cuffs close vertically with two buttons; on each lapel six buttons grouped 1 – 2 – 3.
White waistcoat and breeches.

Regiment van Saxen-Gotha, raised 1744 (1st Battalion on the Zeeland establishment, 2nd Battalion on the Friesland establishment).
Inhaber: from 1744 Wilhelm Fürst von Saxe-Gotha, 1749 Friedrich III Herzog von Saxe-Gotha, 1769 August Fürst von Saxe-Gotha.
In 1806 incorporated as the 3rd Battalion of the 6th Infantry Regiment of the Batavian Republic.
Battles: Siege of Hulst, Siege of Bergen op Zoom.
Uniform in 1747: officer's portrait shows a dark blue coat lined red, with red full cuffs, rounded off lapels, silver buttons. White waistcoat and breeches. Silver shoulder knot and aiguillette on the right shoulder. Hat with silver lace, narrow silver lace loop and orange cockade.

1753: blue coat lined red, with red Swedish style cuffs and lapels, pewter buttons. The lapels are wide at the top and narrow at the bottom, being rounded off.

1766: blue coat lined red, with red Swedish style cuffs, lapels and shoulder strap, blue small standing collar, pewter buttons; lapels have six buttons (three pairs) each.

1768: the cuffs become straight and close vertically with two cuff buttons; a red falling collar is added.

Colour Plate Commentaries

Plate 1: National Infantry, 1715–1740

A. Musketeer, Regiment Van Pallandt, England 1715
The depiction is based on a watercolour in the Gelders Archief, dated several years earlier. The cap (A1 and A2) is after a surviving cap in the collection of the United Services Museum in Edinburgh.

B. Musketeer, Regiment Van Huffel, England 1719
From the painting by Peter Tillemans in the Scottish National Portrait Gallery. Tillemans based his painting on eyewitness accounts and painted it the same year as the battle.

C. Drummer, Regiment Doys, 1731
The manuscript of the drill manual includes two illustrations of recruiting scenes, showing the dress of the officers and drummers in reversed colours. Despite the illustrations being somewhat primitive, they show a lot of details.

4. Officer, Regiment Oranje-Friesland, 1732
After the series of portraits in the Fries Museum Leeuwarden.

Plate 2: Swiss Infantry, 1720–1750

A. Colours of the Swiss regiments, 1743-1748
From *Les Triomphes de Louis XV*.

B. Grenadier, Regiment De Constant-Rebecque, 1748

C. Grenadier, Regiment Hirzel, 1748
David Morier did a series of paintings, not only of grenadiers of all the British regiments, but also from the allied troops. Only a few paintings depict Dutch troops, of which two show each three grenadiers of the Swiss regiments. Both these grenadiers are based on those paintings, showing the slight differences in uniforms and equipment.

D. Musketeer, Regiment Hirzel van Wolflingen, 1726
Based on a reconstruction by Ten Raa; the original painting is sadly lost.

E. Grenadier officer's cap, 1730

F. Officer, Regiment Stürler (2e Regiment Zwitsers van Bern), Germany 1743
Based on the portrait of Lieutenant Colonel De Gumoëns in the
Landesmuseum in Zürich.

Plate 3: Scots Infantry, 1730–1760

A. Musketeer, Regiment Colyear, 1731
Based on a receipt, listing the cloth delivered to the regiment.

B. Musketeer, Regiment Lamy of Dunkenny, 1740
From a copy by Ten Raa of an original watercolour.

C. Musketeer, Regiment Stuart, Rocoux 1746
Based on receipts, listing the delivery of cloth and caps. C1 and C2 show the
bearskin cap worn after 1750.

D. Grenadier, Regiment Gordon, 1758
After a contemporary watercolour.

Plate 4: German and Walloon Infantry, 1740–1760

A. Musketeer, 1e Bataljon van Waldeck, German campaign 1743
Based on contemporary images of musketeers and a schematic order of battle
of the army in 1743.

B. Officer, Regiment Saxe Gotha, Bergen op Zoom 1747
Based on a watercolour by Ten Raa, after an original painting.

C. Grenadier, Walloon Regiment, Bergen op Zoom 1747
Morier painted a grenadier of the Walloon Regiment, together with a
grenadier of the Schwarzburg-Rudolstadt Regiment, perhaps because both
are in blue and white uniforms. The latter was hired from the German
principality in 1748.

D. Musketeer, 2e Bataljon van Waldeck, 1756
Based on the illustration in the *Jassenboekje*.

Plate 5: National Infantry, 1750–1770

A. Musketeer, Regiment Van Stolberg, 1758

B. Musketeer, Regiment Evertsen, 1762

C. Musketeer, Regiment Holstein-Gottorp, 1766

D. Musketeer, Regiment Van Randwijck, 1768
All uniforms based on the *Jassenboekje* and contemporary images of musketeers. After 1766, the uniforms followed the Prussian example, making the uniforms tighter. The hats were also reduced in size.

Plate 6: Infantry Companies, 1745–1770

A. Musketeer of a Vrij Compagnie, Maastricht 1747
Of the few paintings by Morier of the Dutch troops, two depict musketeers from the Vrij Compagnieën. One shows three musketeers, whilst the other, painted after 1755, shows an engagement between French troops and a detachment of a Vrij Compagnie, the latter on which this reconstruction is based.

B. Officer, Amsterdam Marine Company, 1760
From the portrait of Captain Dirk Trip.

C. Drummer, Compagnie Gardes Friesland, 1765
From a contemporary print in the collection of the Rijksmuseum, after which Boode made a reconstruction.

D. Sergeant, Compagnie Invaliden, 1766
Based on the description in the *Jassenboekje*.

Bibliography

Contemporary Regulations

'Geredresseerde Ordre op de Exercitie van de Militie'; 1688 Jacobus Scheltus, ordinaris Drucker ten dienste van sijne Hoogheyt den Heere Prince van Orange, woonende op het Binnenhof, 's Gravenhage.

'Ordre en Woorden van Commando, op de handelingen van de Snaphaan […]'; 1701 Jacobus Scheltus, ordinaris Drucker ten dienste van sijne Koninghlijcke Majesteyt van Groot Brittanien, 's Gravenhage.

'Recueil des Ordonnances Militaires de Sa Majesté Brittanique et des Seigneurs Etats Generaux des Provinces-Unies des Païs-Bas, pour le Reglement des Troupes qui sont au Service de Leurs Hautes Puissances. Seconde Edition'; 1708 Paul Scheltus, Imprimeur Ordinaire de Leurs Hautes Puissances et Henri van Bulderen, Marchand Libraire, dans Le Pooten, 's Gravenhage.

'Reglementen voor de Militie van den Staat der Vereenighde Nederlanden […]'; 1728 Paulus Scheltus, ordinaris Drucker van de Edele Mog. Heeren Raaden van Staate der Vereenighde Nederlanden, 's Gravenhage.

'Geredresseerde Ordre op de handeling van de Snaphaan, benevens de Explicatie beginnende wanneer dezelve op Schouder gehouden werd met de Bajonnet op de Loop'; 1749 Isaac en Jacobus Scheltus, ordinaris Drukker van Zyne Hoogheid, 's Gravenhage.

'Recueil van Verscheidene Placaaten, Ordonantien, Resolutien, Instructien, Ordres en Lysten, &c. Betreffende de saaken van OORLOG, soo te Waater als te Lande', part IV. 1749 Jacobus Scheltus, 's Lands Drukker, The Hague.

'Reglement en Generaele Ordres voor de Regimenten Infanterie van den Staat', 1772 Isaac Scheltus, ordinaris Drukker van Zyne Hoogheid, 's-Gravenhage.

Archival Sources

Bibliothèque nationale de France, département Estampes et photographie, PET FOL-ID-41.

'Les Triomphes de Louis 14, dit Le Grand, Roy de France & de Navarre, Representés par les Drapeaux, Gindons et Etandards qui ont été pris sur les Ennemis de Sa Majesté, dans les batailles, et recontres, et prises de villes, et qui ont été apportes en ceremonie dans l'Eglise de Notre Dame de Paris depuis 1674 jusqu'à la fin de son Régne'.

Bibliotheque nationale de France, département Estampes et photographie, FOL-ID-46., 'Les Triomphes de Louis Quinze, Roy de France & de Navarre'.

Nationaal Militair Museum, Soesterberg, 'Orde und worter von Commando auf die Handgriffe vom Schnapphaan vor einen Musquetier, neben die vor Grenediers und Piekeniers exercition alles nebens derselber Explication in orde gebragt'. 1730 manuscript by E.W. Bilderbeek.

Nationaal Militair Museum, Soesterberg, 'Album 8: Vaandels van het Staatse Leger (18^e en 19^e
eeuw)'; 'Album 11: Nederlandse Infanterieuniformen omstreeks 1700'; 'Album 13: 18^e eeuw
uniformen, o.a. Grenadiers, Cavalerie'. Uniform documentation by F.G. de Wilde

Published Sources

Anon., *Beknopte Historie van t Vaderland, van de vroegste tijden af tot aan het jaar 1767*, Part 3
(Amsterdam: Petrus Conradi,1787).

Anon, *Nauwkeurig Dag-verhaal van 't Campement by Oosterhout* (The Hague: Adriaan Moetjens,
Boekverkoper, 1732).

Anon, *Nederlandsch Gedenkboek of Europische Mercurius, berigtende De Gesteltenissen der
Zaaken van Staat en Oorlog, in alle Heerschappijen en Landschappen van Europa, beneevens
d'aangrenzende gewesten*, (53rd edition) ('s-Gravenhage: Fredric Henric Scheurleer, 1752).

Bosscha, J., *Neêrlands Heldendaden te Land, van de vroegste tijden af tot in onze dagen* Part 2
(Leeuwarden: G.T.N. Sturingar, 1838).

Bosscher, Drs. Ph.M., *De Nederlandse Mariniers* (Bussum: Van Dishoeck, Van Holkema en
Warendorf N.V., 1966).

Busscher, Meinhard, Rev., *Opwekking en Anmoediging van Neerlant, om zig (met God) kloekelijk
te verdedigen tegen hare Vianden, in een Dissertatie over 2 Chron. 32: 1–8. Ingesloten met
een Staats- Krygs- en Zedekundig gebruik* (Groningen: Hajo Spandaw, Boekverkoper in de
Guldenstraat, 1747).

Charrié, Pierre, 'Les Drapeaux des Régiments Suisses au Service des Pays Bas pendant la Campagne
de Flandre, 1745–1747', lecture (transcript) in *Proceedings of the 15th International Congress of
Vexillology, 23–27 August 1993* (Zürich: Swiss Society of Vexillology, 1993).

Daenen, J.S.M., Th.R. Kraus en J.H.V. Notermans, *Thans bonst het grof geschut... De verovering en
bezetting van Maastricht in 1748* (Maastricht: Maastricht Stichting Historische Reeks, 2001).

Dekkers, R.M., G.J. Johannes and L.C. van de Pol (eds.), *De Bredasche Heldinne* (Hilversum:
Verloren B.V., 1988).

Dibbetz, Johan, *Het Groot Militair Woordenboek [...]* ('s-Gravenhage: Jacobus van den Kieboom,
1740).

Ferguson, James (ed.), *Papers illustrating the history of the Scots Brigade in the service of the United
Netherlands 1572–1782*, Volume II (Edinburgh: Scottish History Society, 1899).

Grossfeldt, R., *De 'Kleine Oorlog'- Over de ontwikkeling van de lichte troepen, 1740–1790*, graduate
thesis for the Faculty of Humanities; Utrecht University, 2011.

Hoof, Joep van (ed.), *Nederlandse Militaire Uniformen, 1752–1800* (The Hague: Netherlands
Institute for Military History, 2011).

Meier, Jürg A., *Vivat Hollandia. Zur Geschichte der Schweizer in holländischen Diensten 1740–1795
Griffwaffen und Uniformen* (Lingenfeld: Maierdruck, 2008),

Nimwegen, Dr. Olaf van, *Dien Fatalen Dag, Het beleg van Bergen op Zoom 1747*(Bergen op Zoom:
Sector Archiefzaken Bergen op Zoom, in coöperation with Van der Kreek and Quist book
sellers, 1997).

Nimwegen, Dr. Olaf van, *De Republiek der Verenigde Nederlanden als Grote Mogendheid –
Buitenlandse politiek en oorlogvoering in de eerste helft van de achttiende eeuw en in het
bizonder tijdens de Oostenrijkse Successieoorlog (1740 – 1748)* (Amsterdam: De Bataafsche
Leeuw, 2002).

Oebschelwitz, L.F.M. von, *Hedendaagsche Krygshandel van de Infantery; of Korte Verhandeling over
derzelver Samenstelling, Wapenrusting,Exercitien, Evolutien en Manoeuvres'; Betrekkelyk tot
alle derzelver eigentlyke Verrichtingen en gantschen Dienst te Velde, Gelyk hedendaags, bij de*

Welgeregeldste Legers waargenomen wordt. [...] (The Hague: Pieter Gerard van Balen, Boek-, Konst- en Kaartverkoper in de Spuystraat, 1761)

Pijnen, F., 'Putte en de Oorlogsperikelen A. D. 1747', in *Tijding – Kroniek van de heemkundekring 't Zuiderkwartier*(Ossendrecht; Tijding, 1985).

Ringoir, H., *De Nederlandse Infanterie* (Bussum: Van Dishoeck, Van Holkema en Warendorf N.V., 1968).

Bedford, John Russel, Duke of, *Correspondence of John, Fourth Duke of Bedford: selected from the originals at Woburn Abbey* Volume I (London: Longman, Brown, Green and Longmans, 1842).

Seters, W.H. van, 'Het Campement bij Oosterhout anno 1732', in *Jaarboek van de Geschied- en Oudheidkundige Kring van Stad en Land van Breda `De Oranjeboom' deel XXII* (Breda: De Oranjeboom, 1969).

Smits, Marjan, & Vogel, Hans (eds.), *Een oorlogsman van dezen tijd en beminnaar der sexe – De autobiografie van Casimir graaf von Schlippenbach (1682–1755)* (Amsterdam: Uitgeverij Augustus, 2007).

Zwitser, H.L., *Het Staatse Leger deel IX, de Achttiende Eeuw 1713–1795* (Amsterdam: De Bataafsche Leeuw, 2012).

Magazine and Journal Articles

Bas, W.G. de, 'Het Campement bij Oosterhout', *De Militaire Spectator* (1916).

Sloot, R.B.F. van der, ''s Lands geweerfabriek te Culemborg', *Armamentaria* 8 (1973).

Wilde, F.G. de, 'Grenadiersmutsen in het Staatse leger', *Armamentaria* 15 (1981).

Wilde, F.G. de, 'De Uniformen van de Schotse Brigade', *Armamentaria* 15 (1981).

Wilde, F.G. de, 'De ontwikkeling van de Infanterie-uniformen in het Staatse Leger gedurende de 18e eeuw', *Armamentaria* 17 (1983).

Wilde, F.G. de, 'De Cent Suisses van het Stadhouderlijk Hof', *Armamentaria* 25 (1991).

Wilde, F.G. de, 'Onderscheidingstekenen voor de officieren en onderofficieren in het Staatse Leger tot 1795', *Armamentaria* 25 (1991).

Wilde, F.G. de, 'De uniformering van de Tête de Colonne 1700–1813', *Armamentaria* 28 (1994).

Online Sources

'Dutch Regiments' at http://soldaten.16mb.com/dutreg.htm.

'Nederlands Militair Erfgoed' at http://www.nederlandsmilitairerfgoed.nl/nl/